Postcards from

BROOKLYN

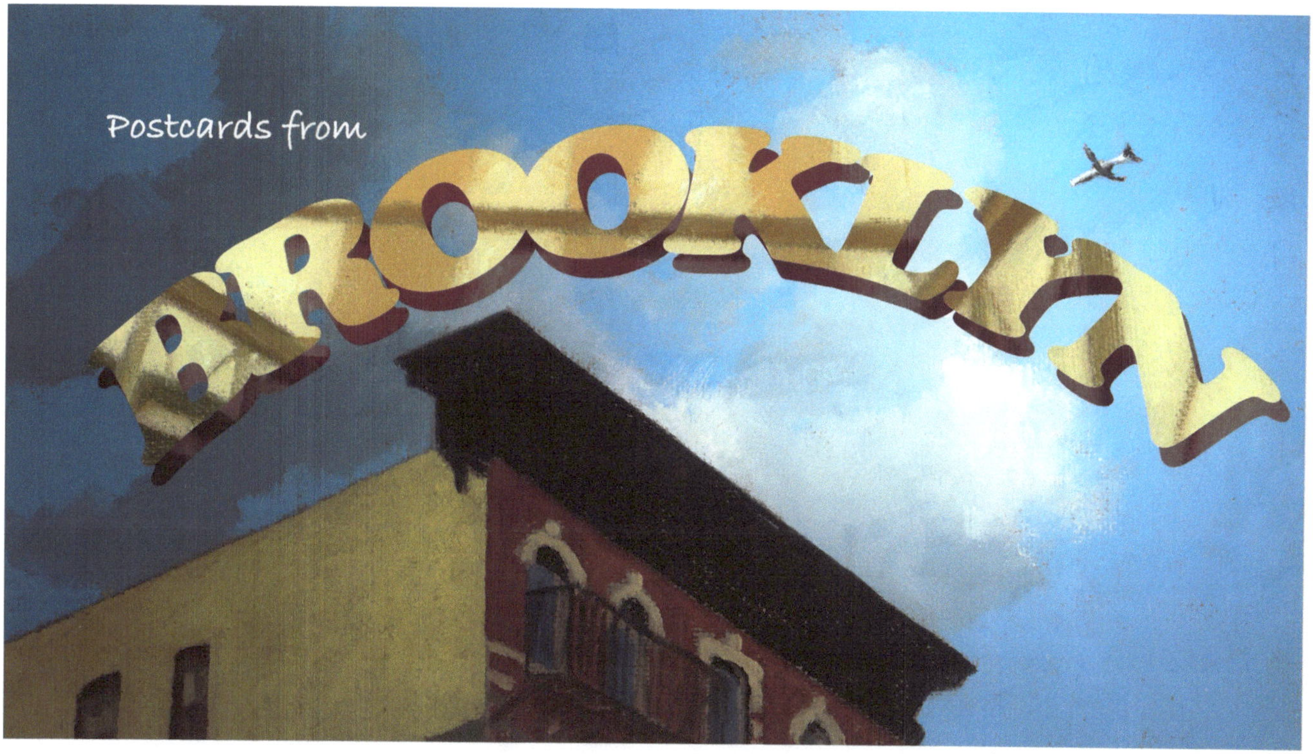

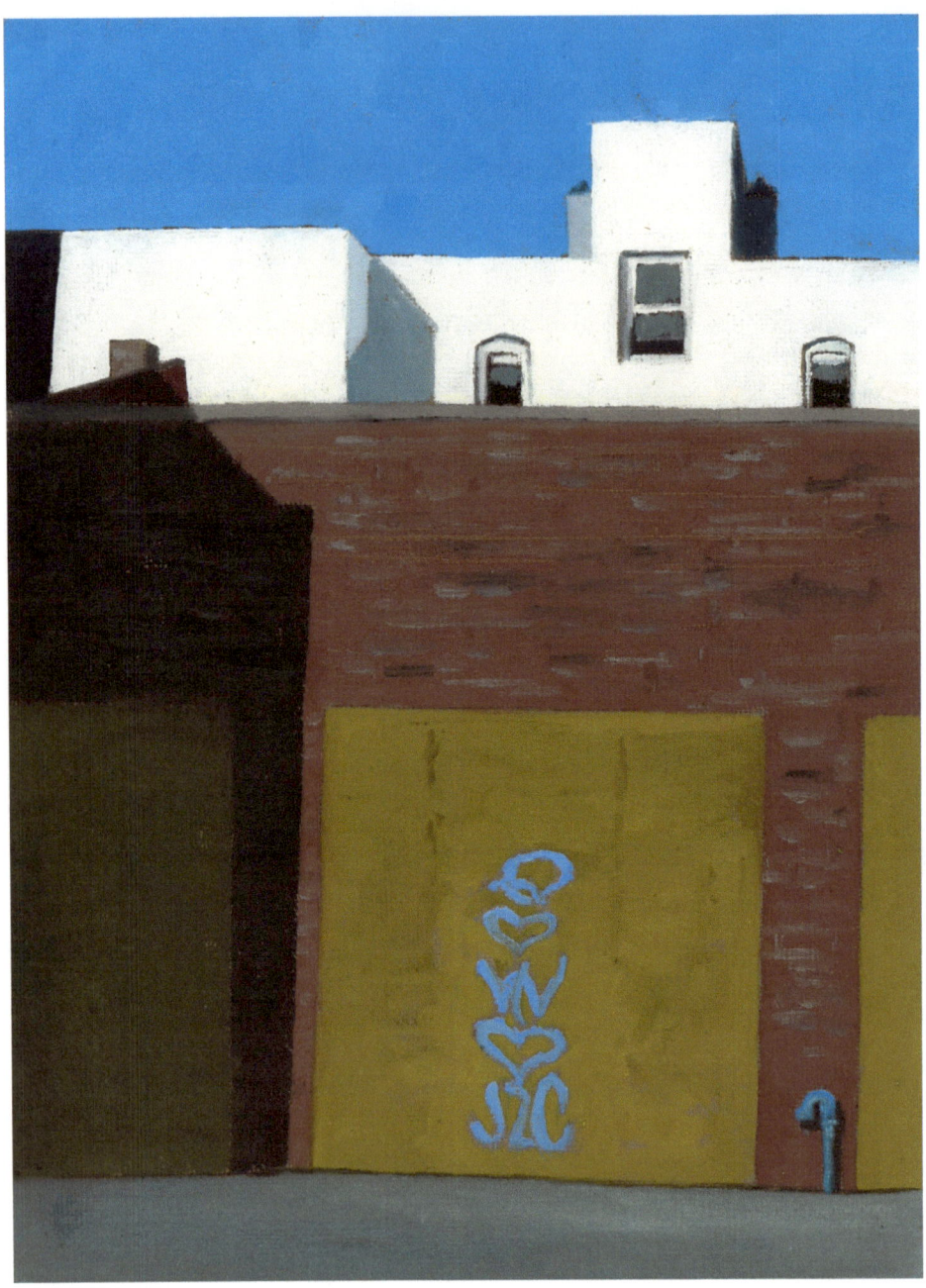

This building looks like it could be from somewhere in the Middle East.  I love the way the pipe matches the graffiti.

Brooklyn was a place I had only dreamt of visiting when my son
and his family moved there in 2004.   I will not forget the first time my husband
and I drove to see my son's new home on Rugby Road in Ditmas Park.
We traveled along Cortelyou Road astonished to see one culture after
another represented in stores, churches and by the many people
busily shopping.

Then we got to Coney Island Road and I realized how close we were
to Coney Island and was again surprised.  The legenday Coney Island
was close by!

As we got closer we passed a huge playing field (The Parade Grounds) with
all kinds of sports going on and I knew they were in the right place
for their growing young boys.  As we got closer  beautiful
Victorian homes in various states of repair filled the neighborhood.
This was not the urban sprall I had imagined at all but a little bit of
heaven.  And so I have, whenever I visited, painted some of the little
pieces of life I found enchanting.

Lured by her brother and his family my daughter decided to move
from San Fransisco to Brooklyn as well.  She settled with her business
in Park Slope.  Here there is another kind of life entirely with
coffee shops restaruants, art galleries, Prospect Park, big old Brownstones
and plenty to do.  Both places are a joy to visit and paint.
What follows is how someone from the burbs of Philly sees Brooklyn.

"Brooklyn was a dream.  All the things that happened there just couldn't happen.  It was all dream stuff.  Or was it all real and true, and it was she Francie that was the dreamer?" from A TREE GROWS IN BROOKLYN

# ROOFTOP DITMAS PARK

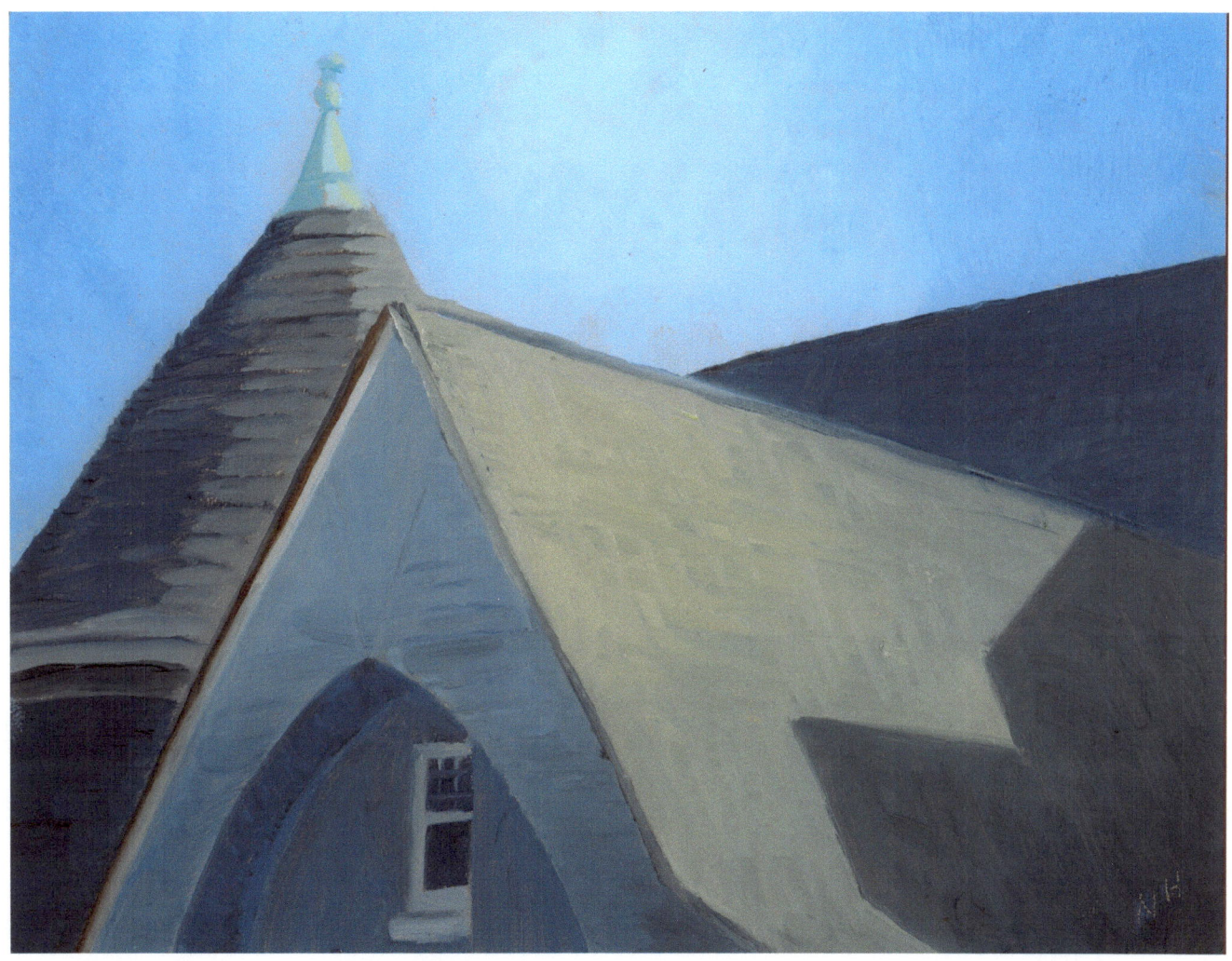

I love the old Victorian houses in Ditmas Park.  This one is a symphony in shades of grey.  I wonder who lives at the top.

# EARLY MORNING IN DITMAS PARK

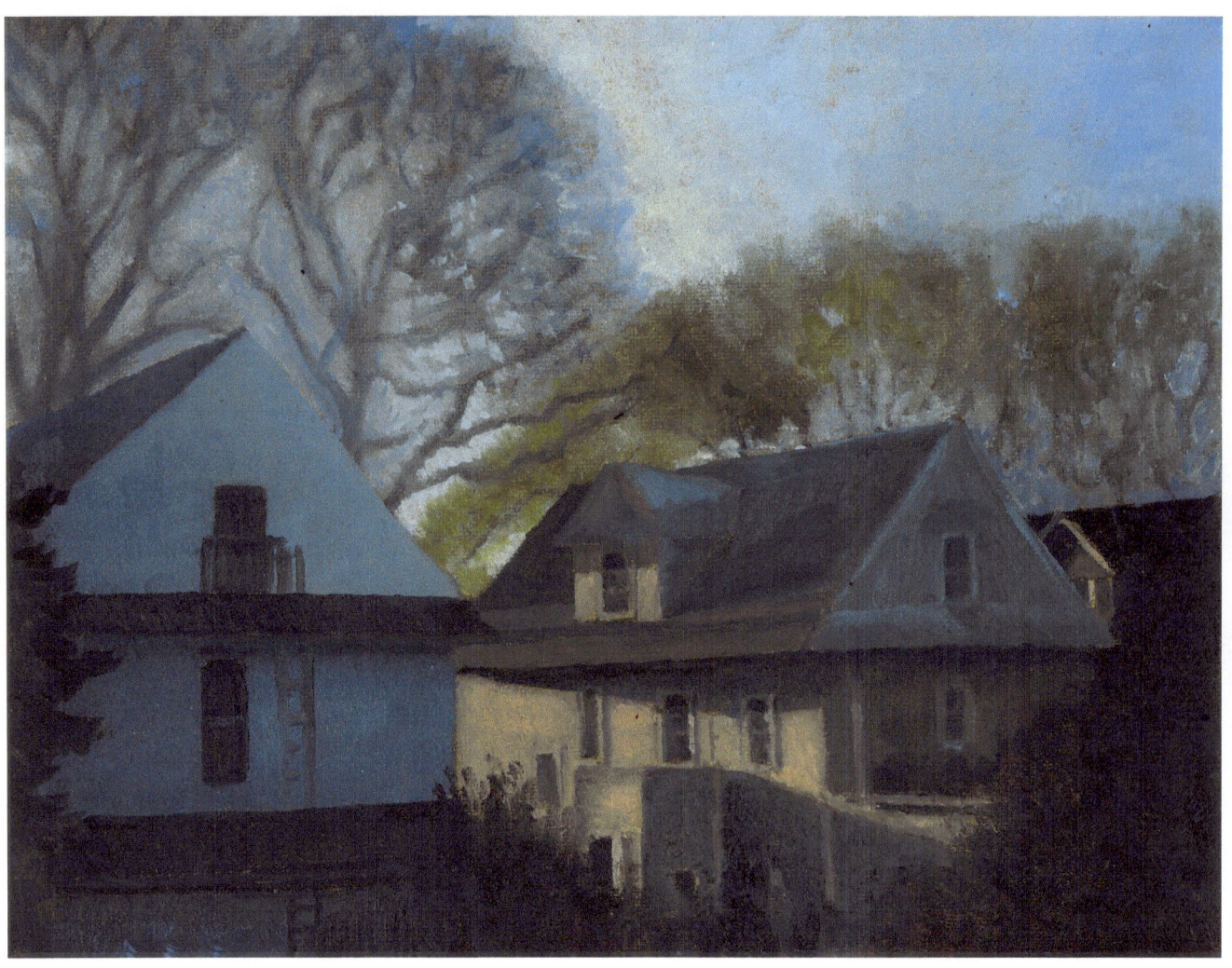

Out my bedroon window I spied this shaft of light that I could not resist.

# OUT THE WINDOW IN DITMAS PARK

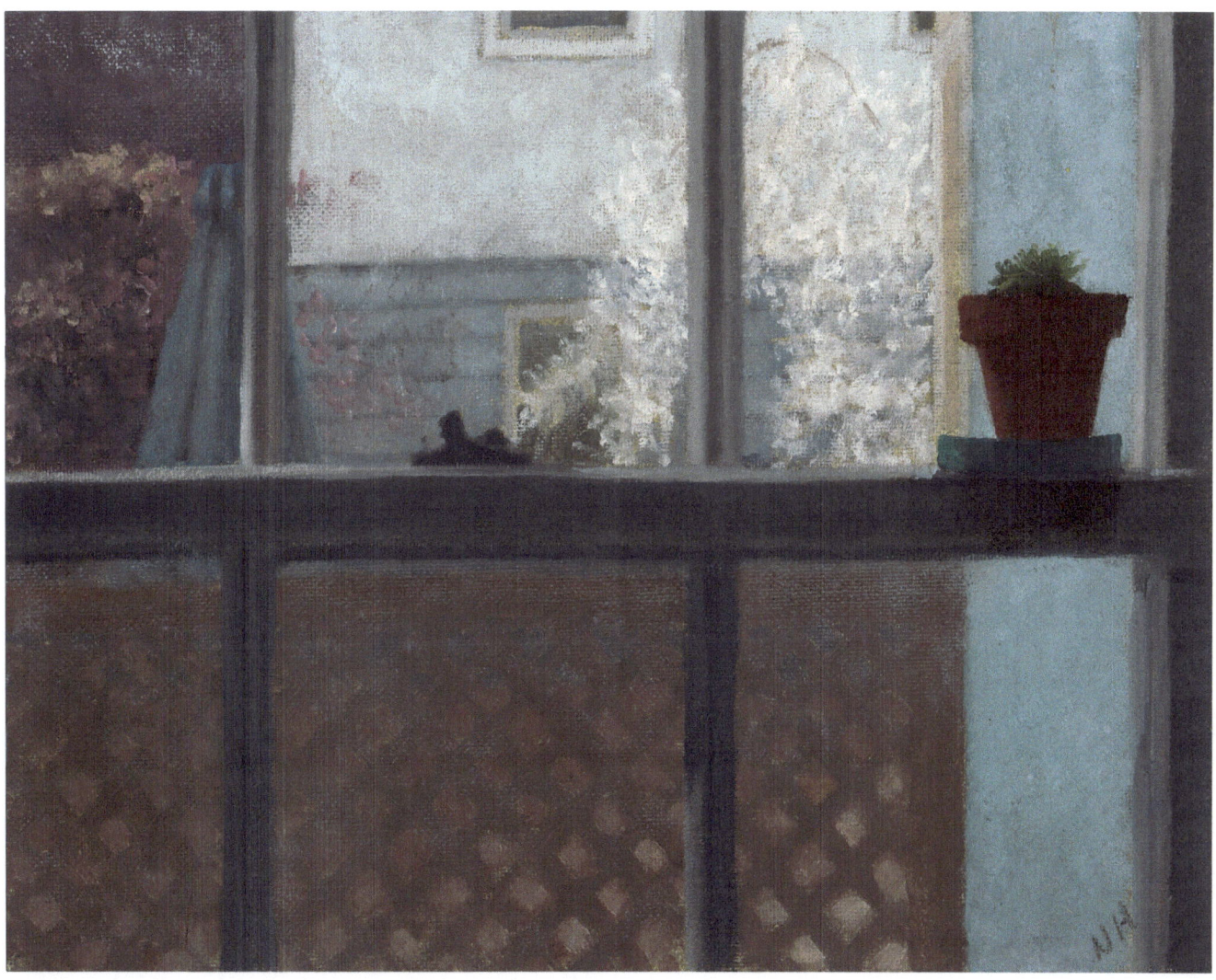

Early spring and everything is blooming. The cherry tree next door has burst forth and even the plant on the window sill has some new green.

# ARGYLE AND ALBEMARLE ROAD

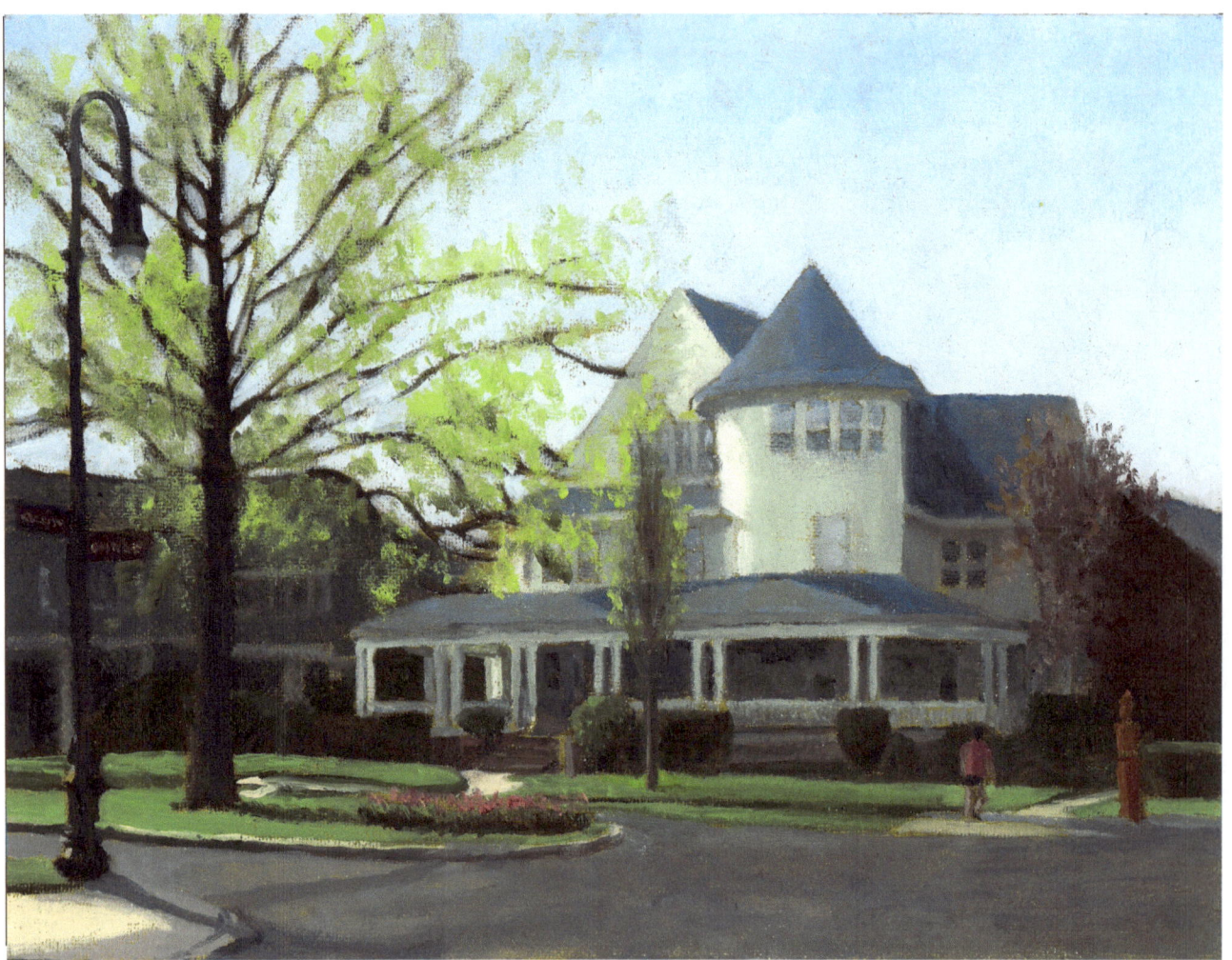

One of the prettiest streets in Brooklyn is Albmarle Road.  It sports a median planted with trees and seasonal flowers.  I am a fan of porches and this one beats all.

# FLATBUSH SWITCH

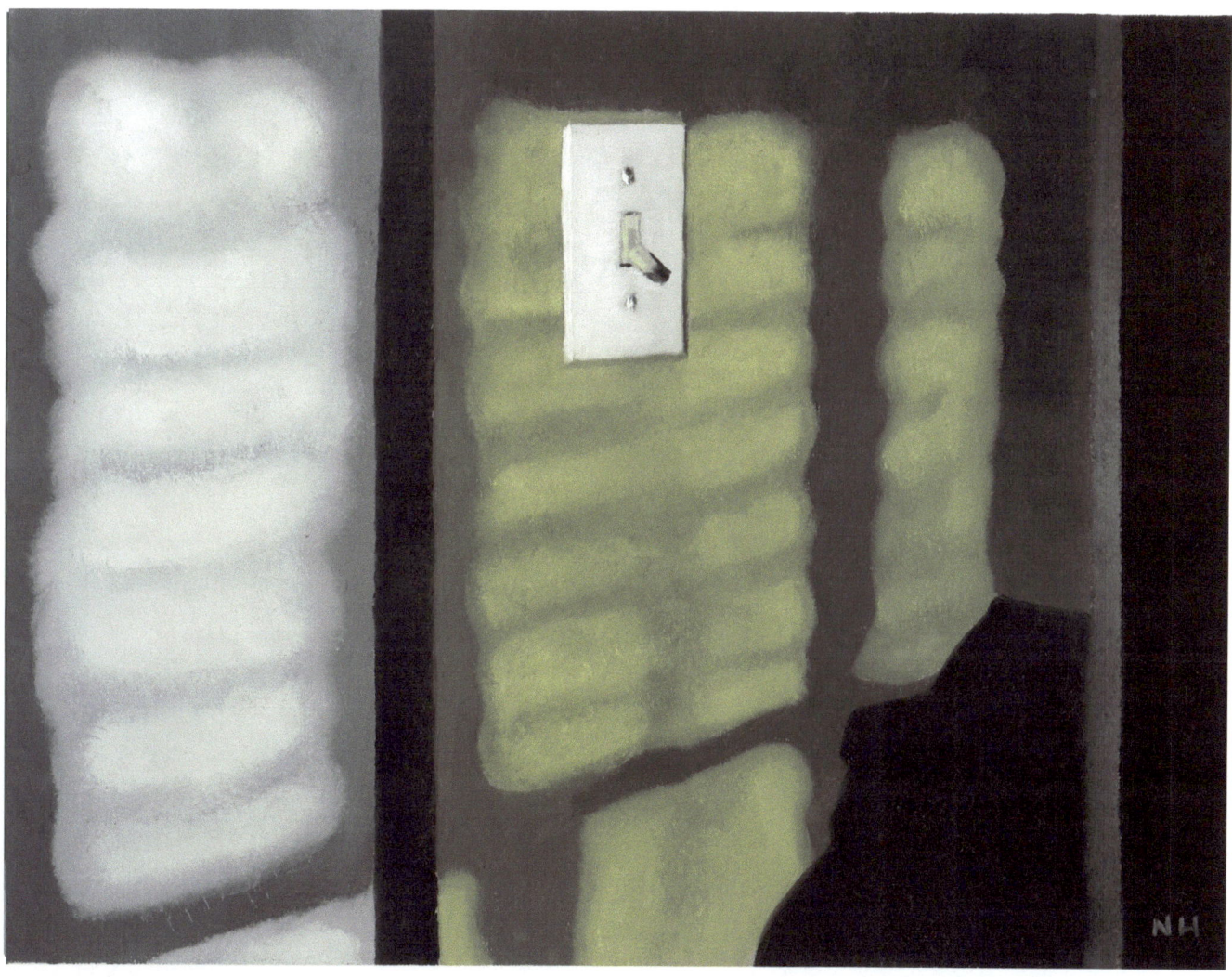

The house is silent, everyone has gone...and then you turn the corner
the light makes a strange pattern and you remember who you are.

Postcards from Brooklyn

ALONE AT THE PARTY

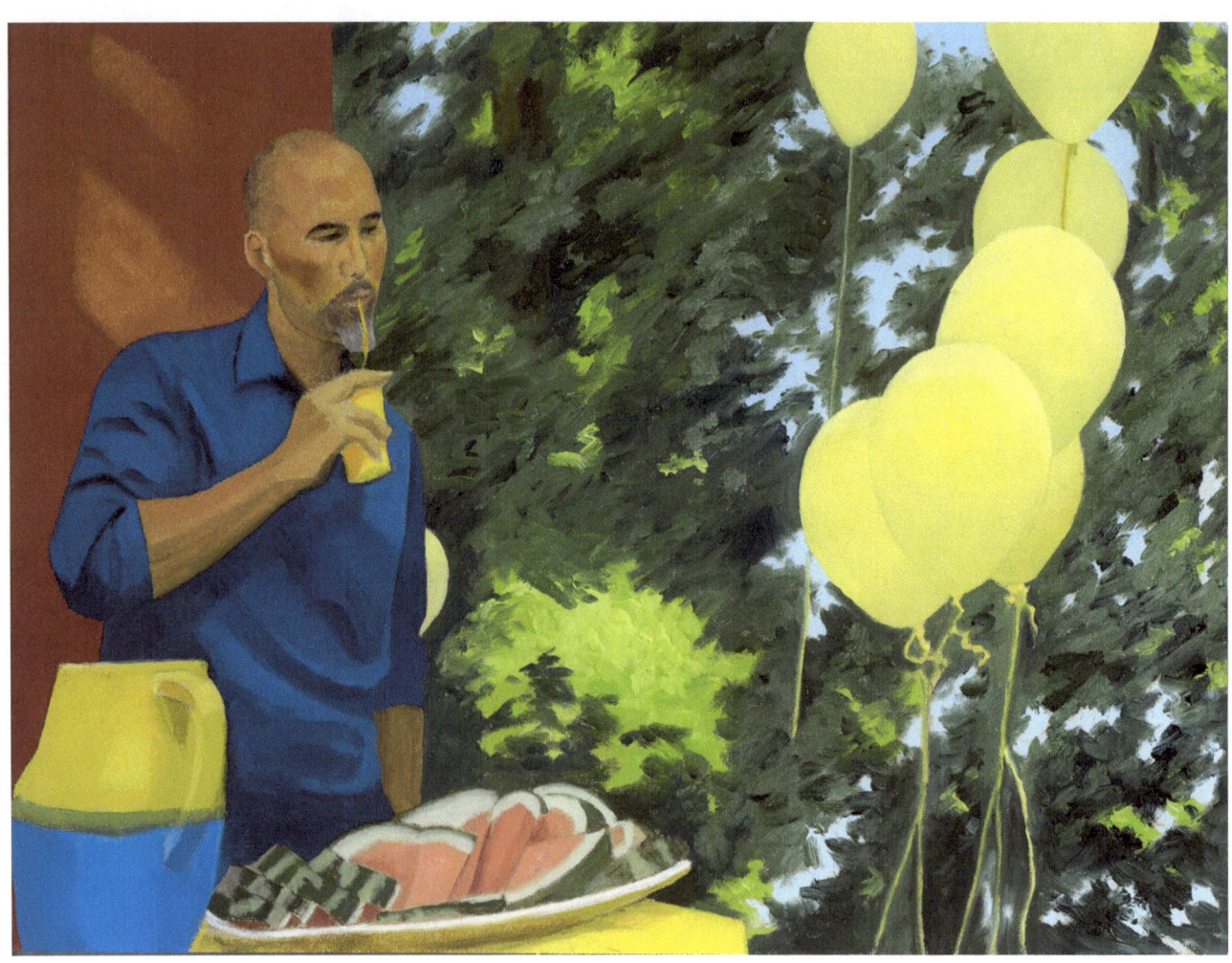

BLUE SHOES

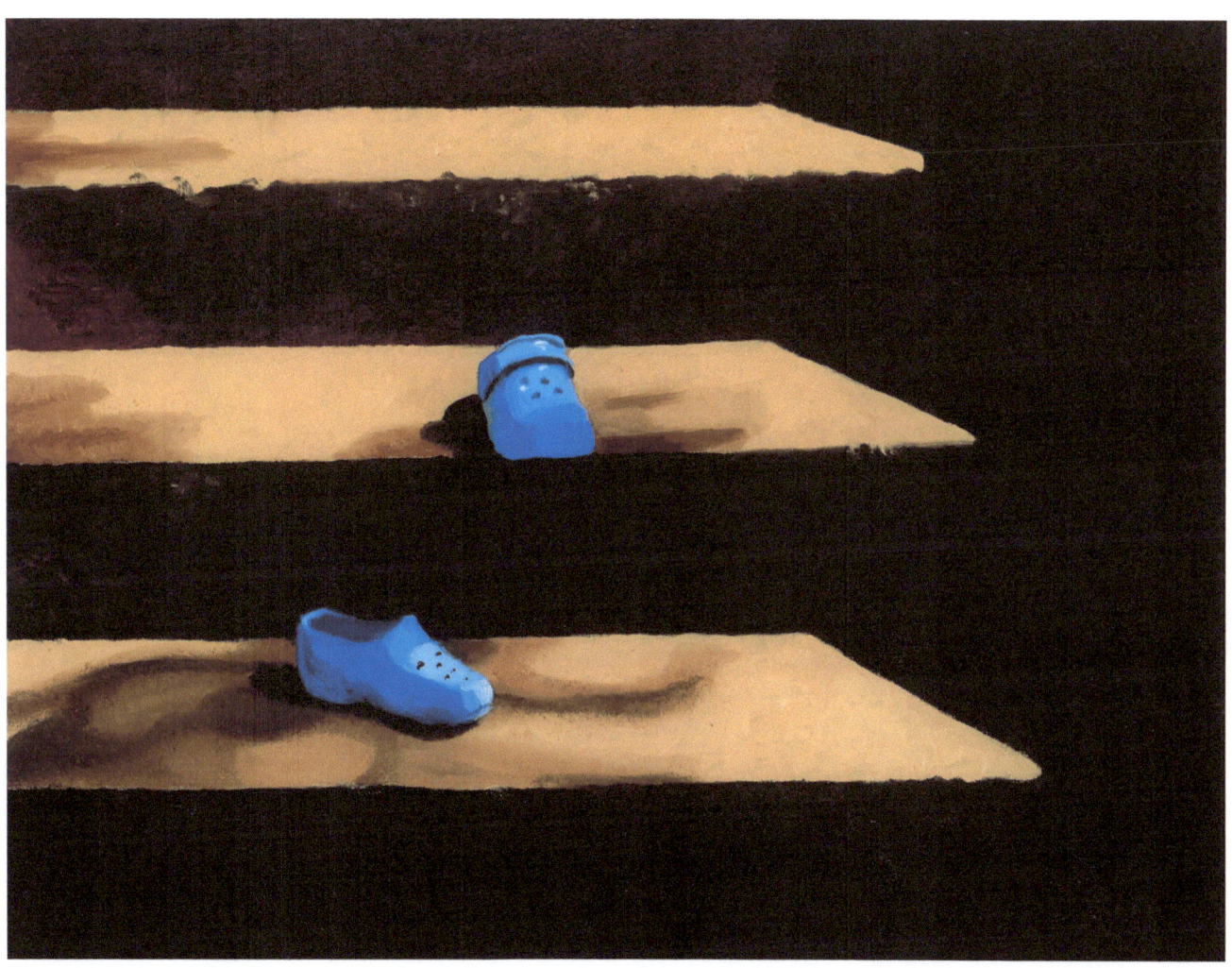

# BROOKLYN VICTORIAN #1

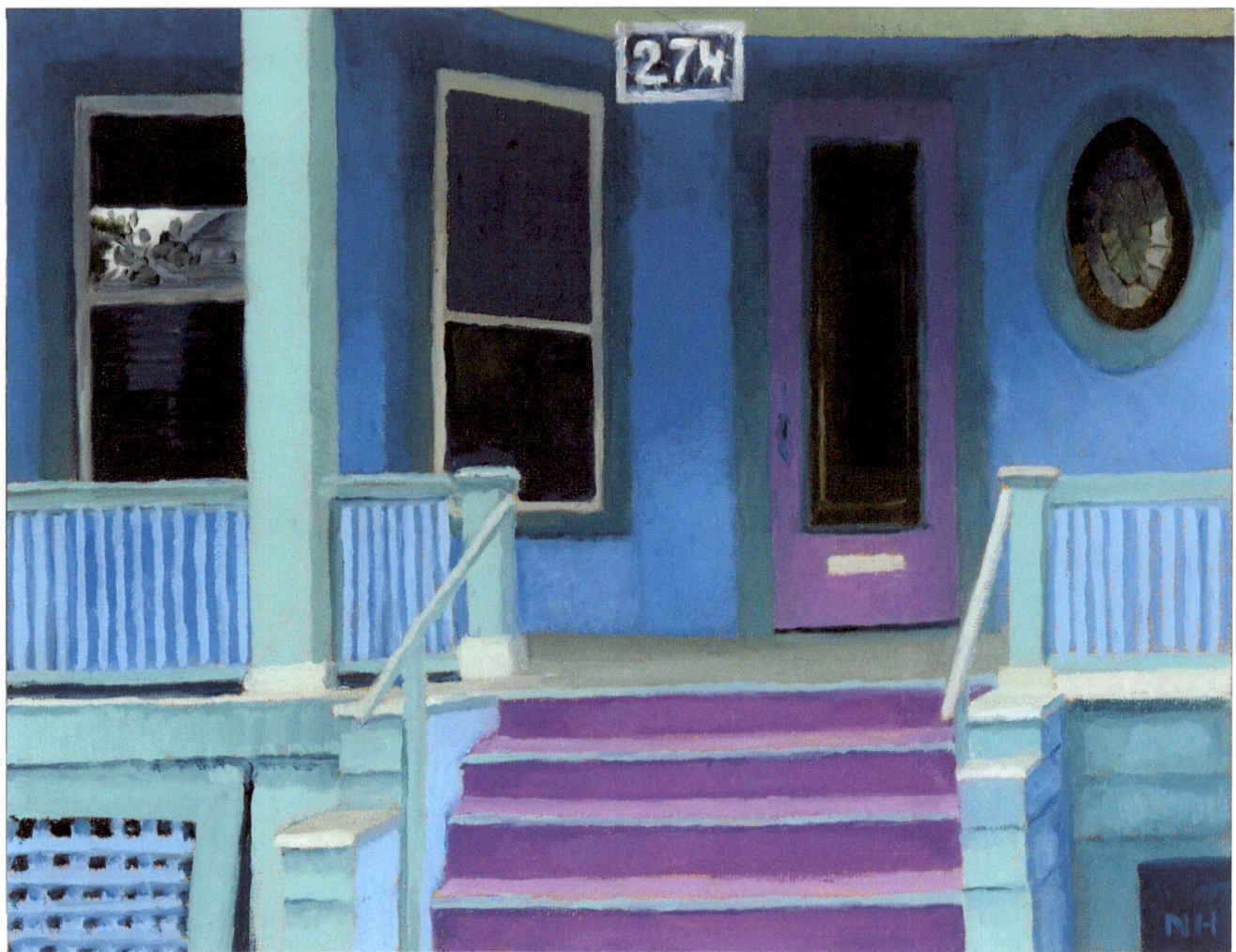

There are a group of Victorian homes in San Francisco that are painted in shades of pink and purple.  They are called "Painted Ladies".
In parts of Flatbush this tradition is exuberantly embraced as in this Rugby Road beauty.

# BROOKLYN VICTORIAN #2

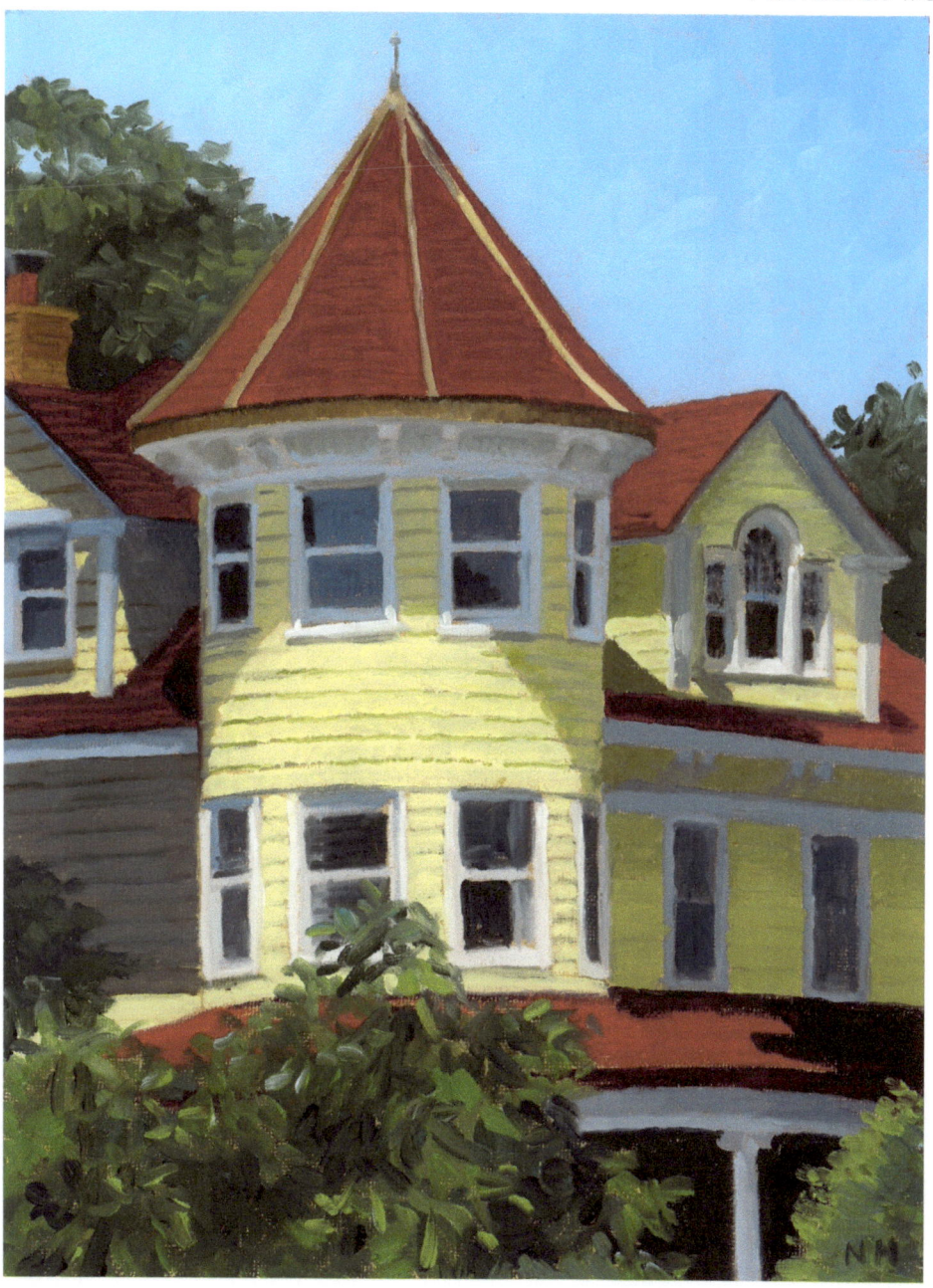

The Ditmas Park Historic District was listed on the National Register of Historic Places in 1983.

# SUNNY RUGBY ROAD

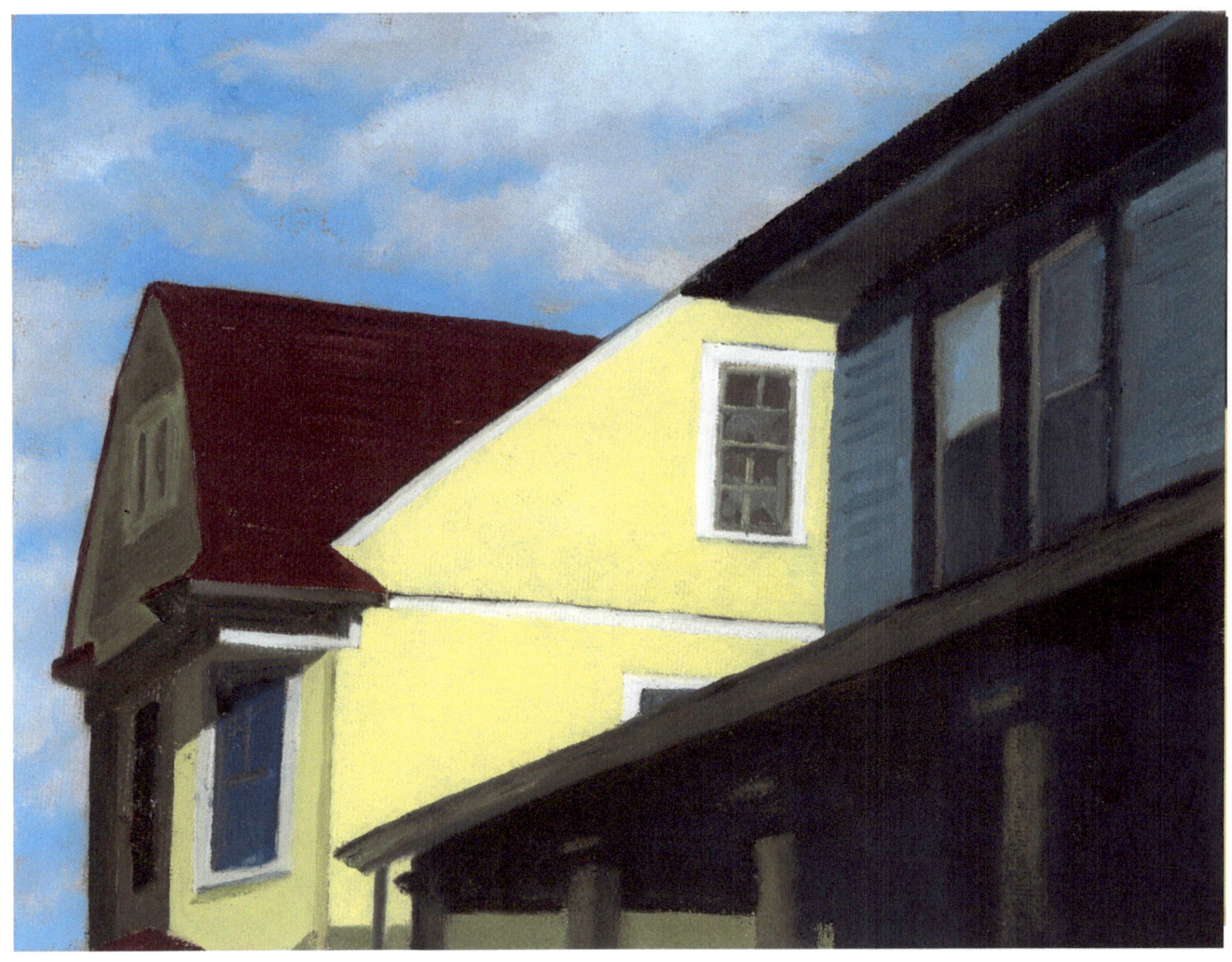

One last painting from Flatbush.

# LOOKING UP

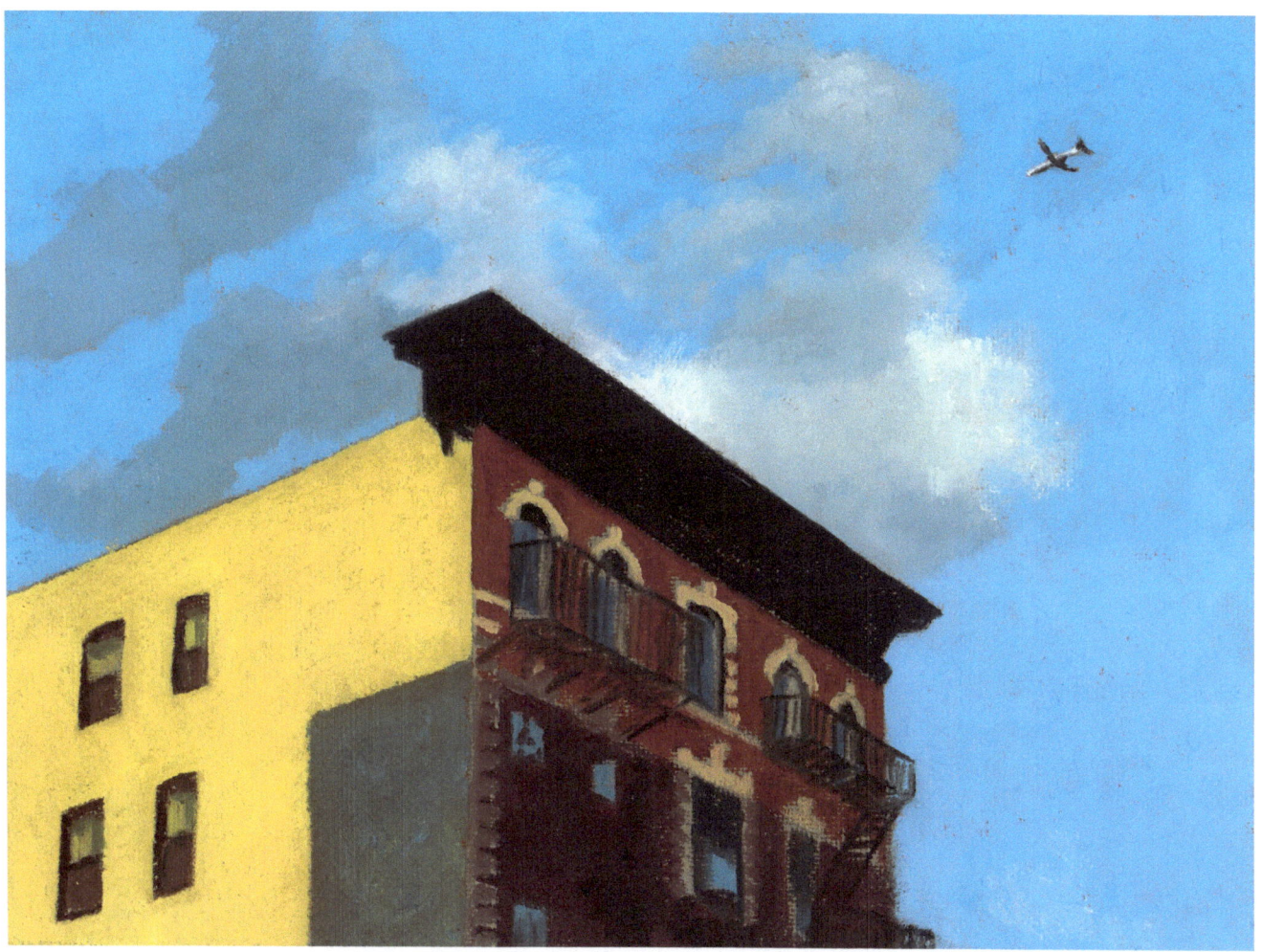

In Park Slope the sun lights up another yellow wall.

# ELLIE IN THE COFFEE SHOP

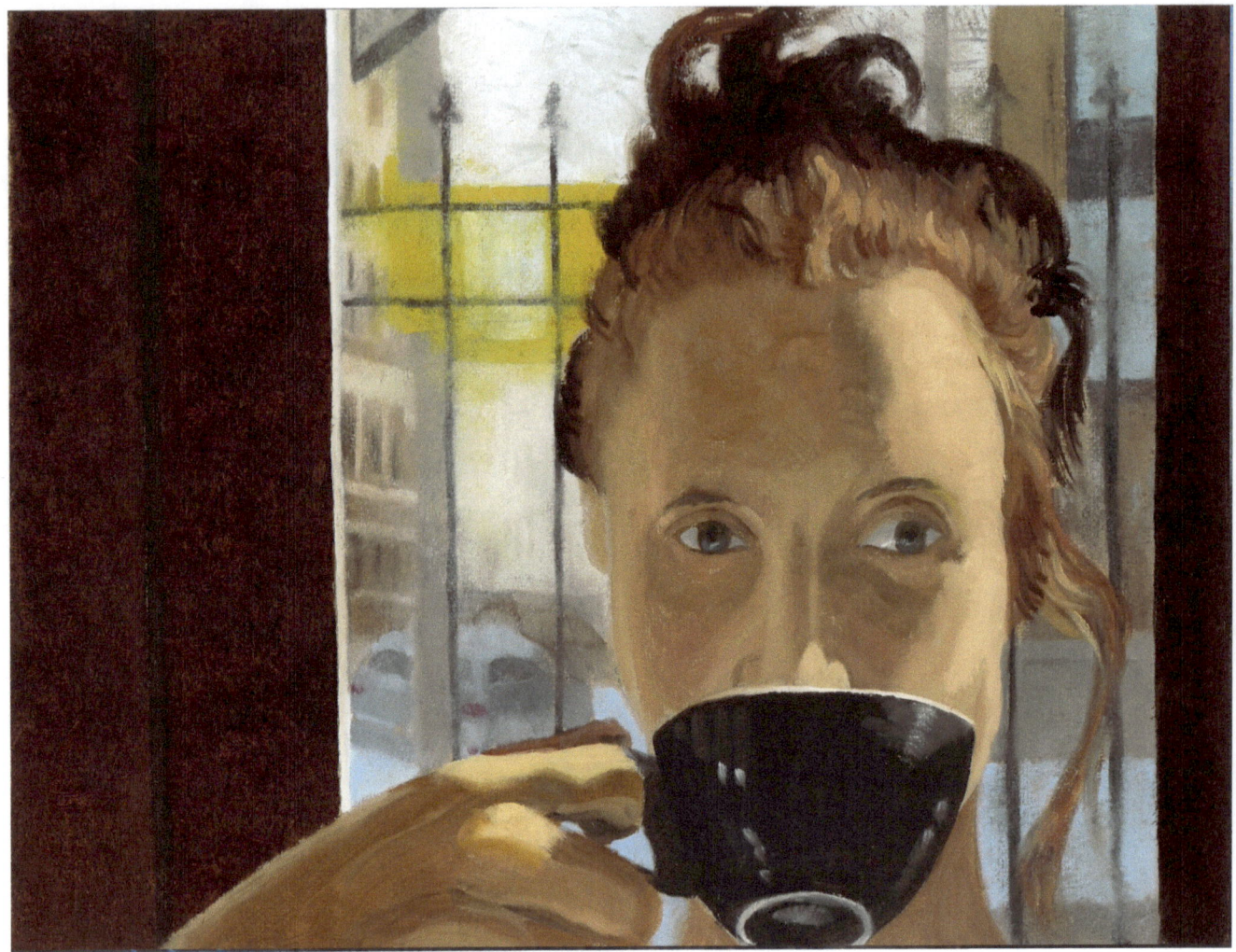

The coffee house has had a real comback in recent years as people bring in their computers and have at least the illusion of company while they work. Back in the 60's, before computers, coffee houses were the place to sing folk songs.

I wonder what would happen if someone took out a guitar today.

# COFFEE HOUSE SUNDAY MORNING

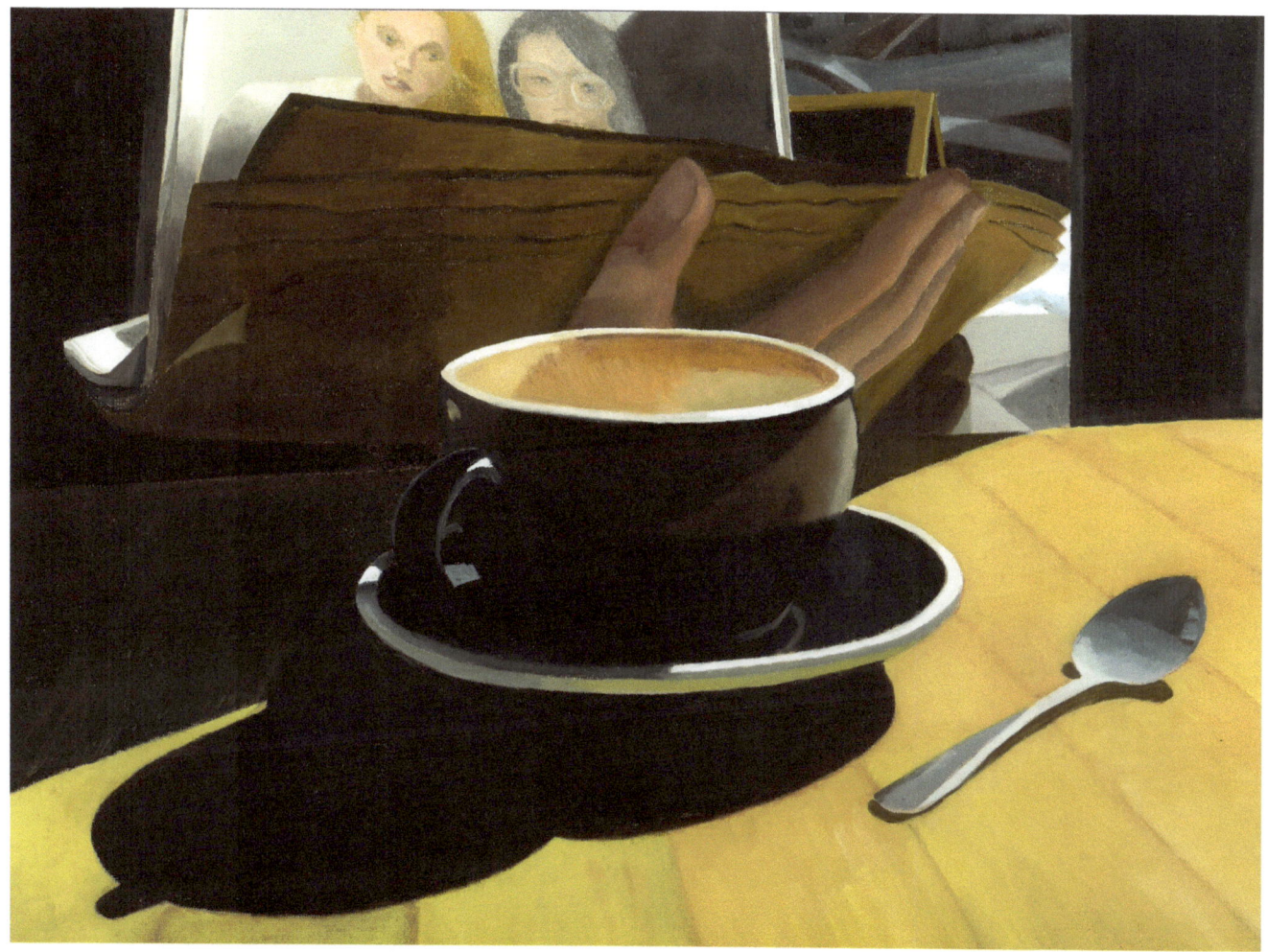

What could be better than a lazy sunny Sunday morning in a friendly coffee shop with the Sunday paper.  First latte finished and not even to the crossword puzzle yet.

# FIRST FLOOR APARTMENT

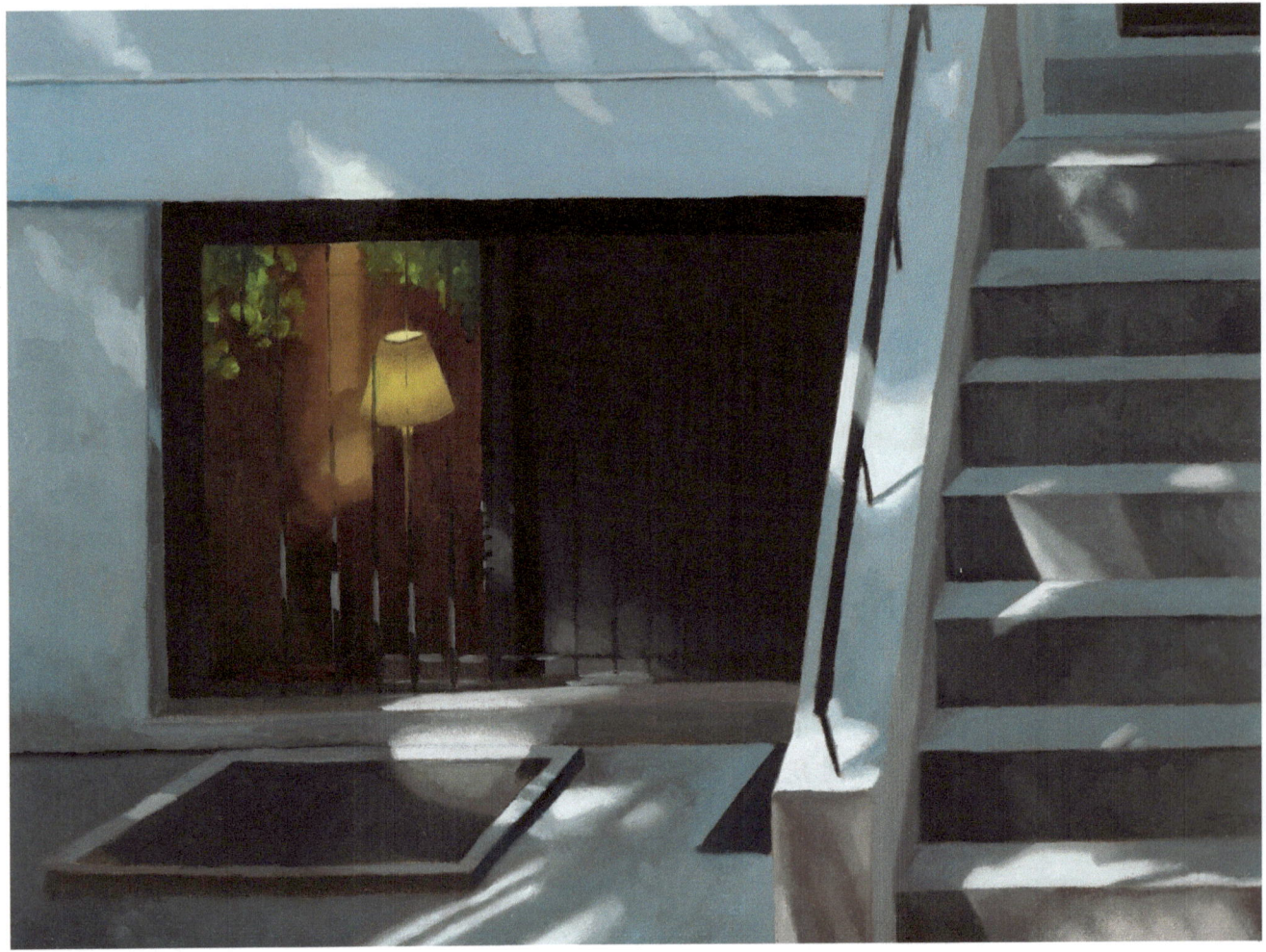

I have always been fascinated by the inside of people's houses.
Rooms without people are an invitation to imagine. For that reason I love to
walk the streets of Park Slope because there it is possible to see into windows
and doorways and imagine what goes on behind the curtains or the bars.
On this sunny day someone has left the light on, or were they reading and
left to answer the phone, or is it a welcoming light for a daytime assignation?

# TIME AND SPACE

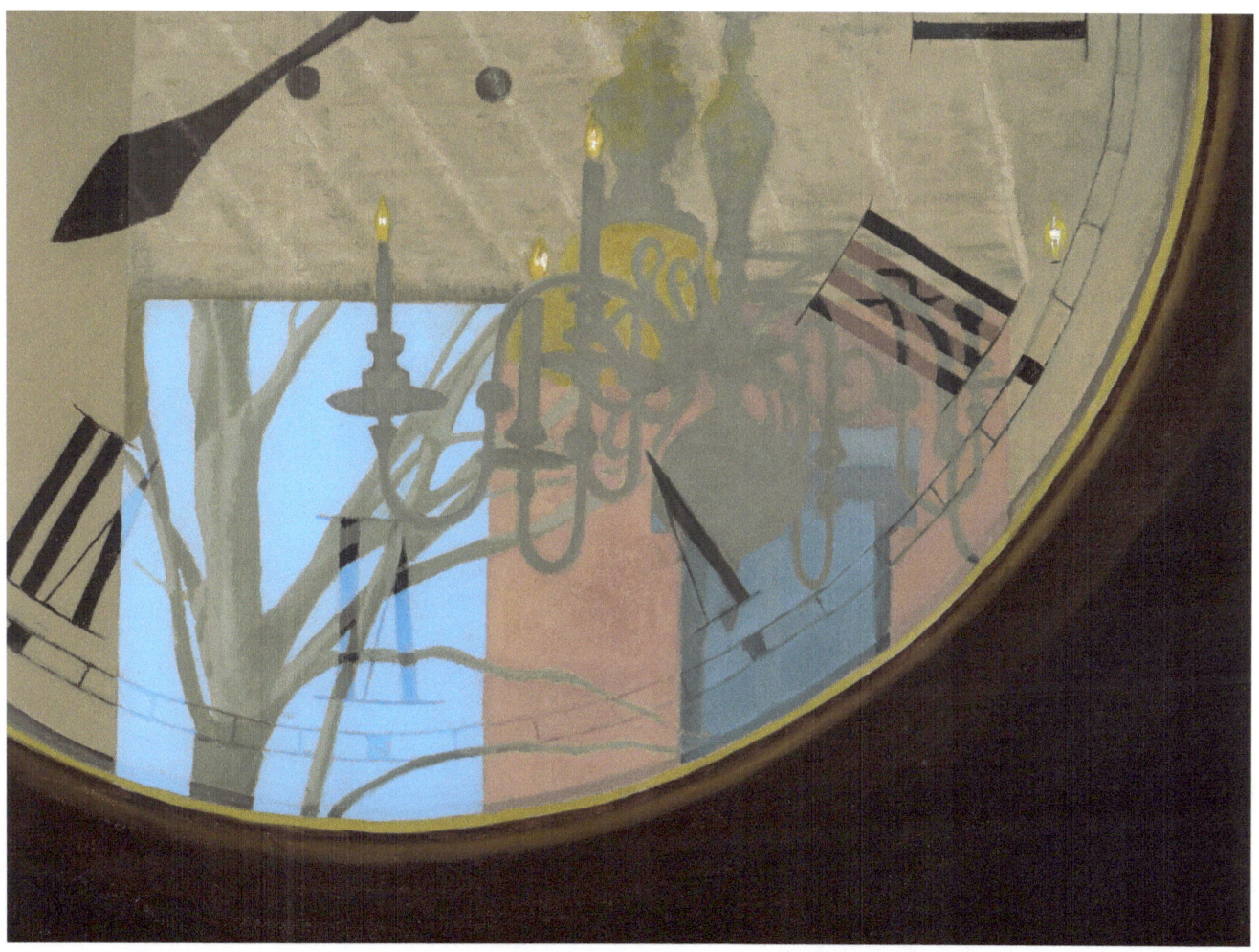

Glass is such a unique surface.  It is transparent and also reflects images.
Is the artist like a piece of glass, revealing some version of reality,
while also showing what's under the surface?

# NEIGHBORS

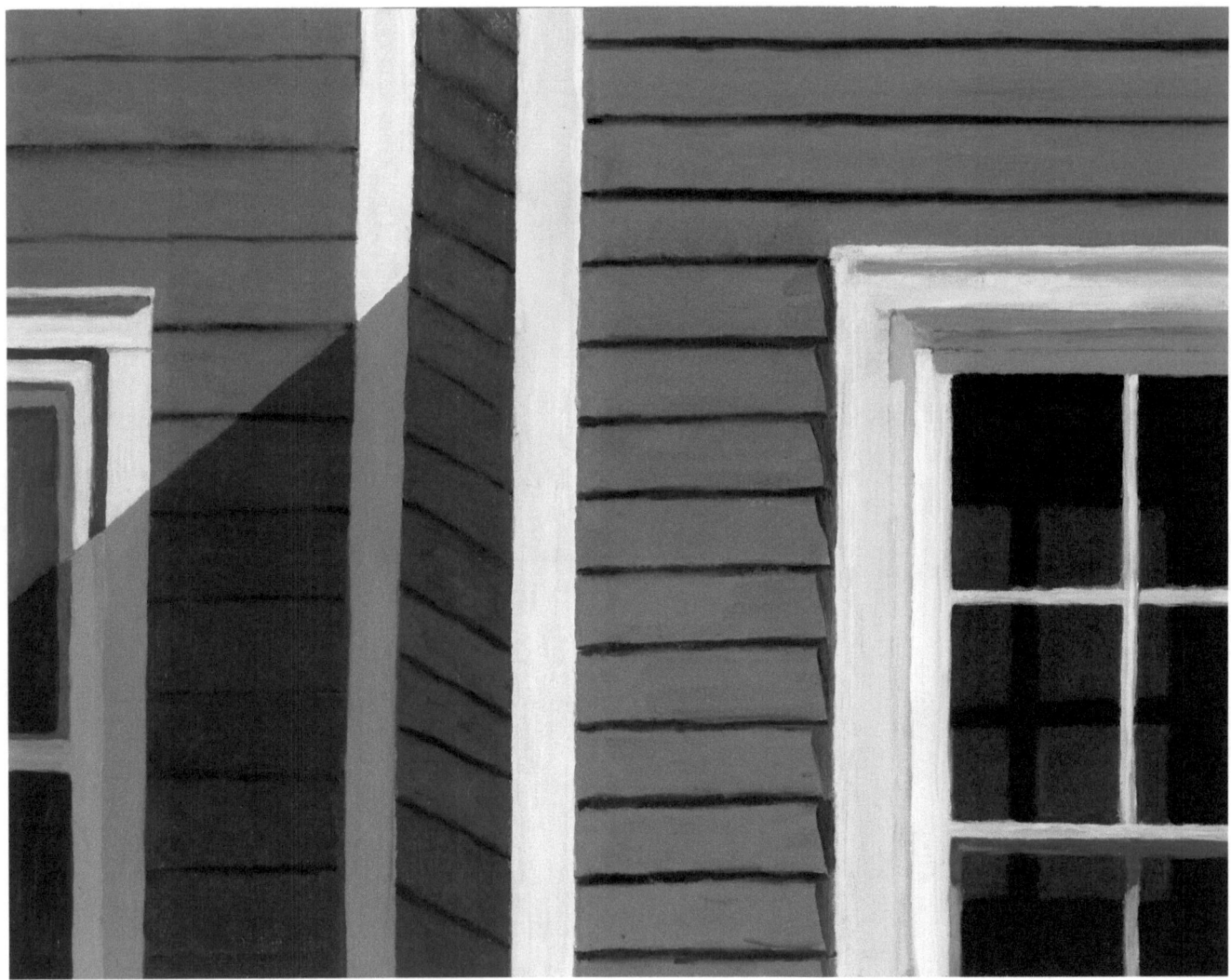

We share our small place on earth with a very few people. All the most basic human interactions begin between neighbors.
In this painting there is a small separation between houses. Is this a composition in white, gray and siena, or a meditation on that separation?

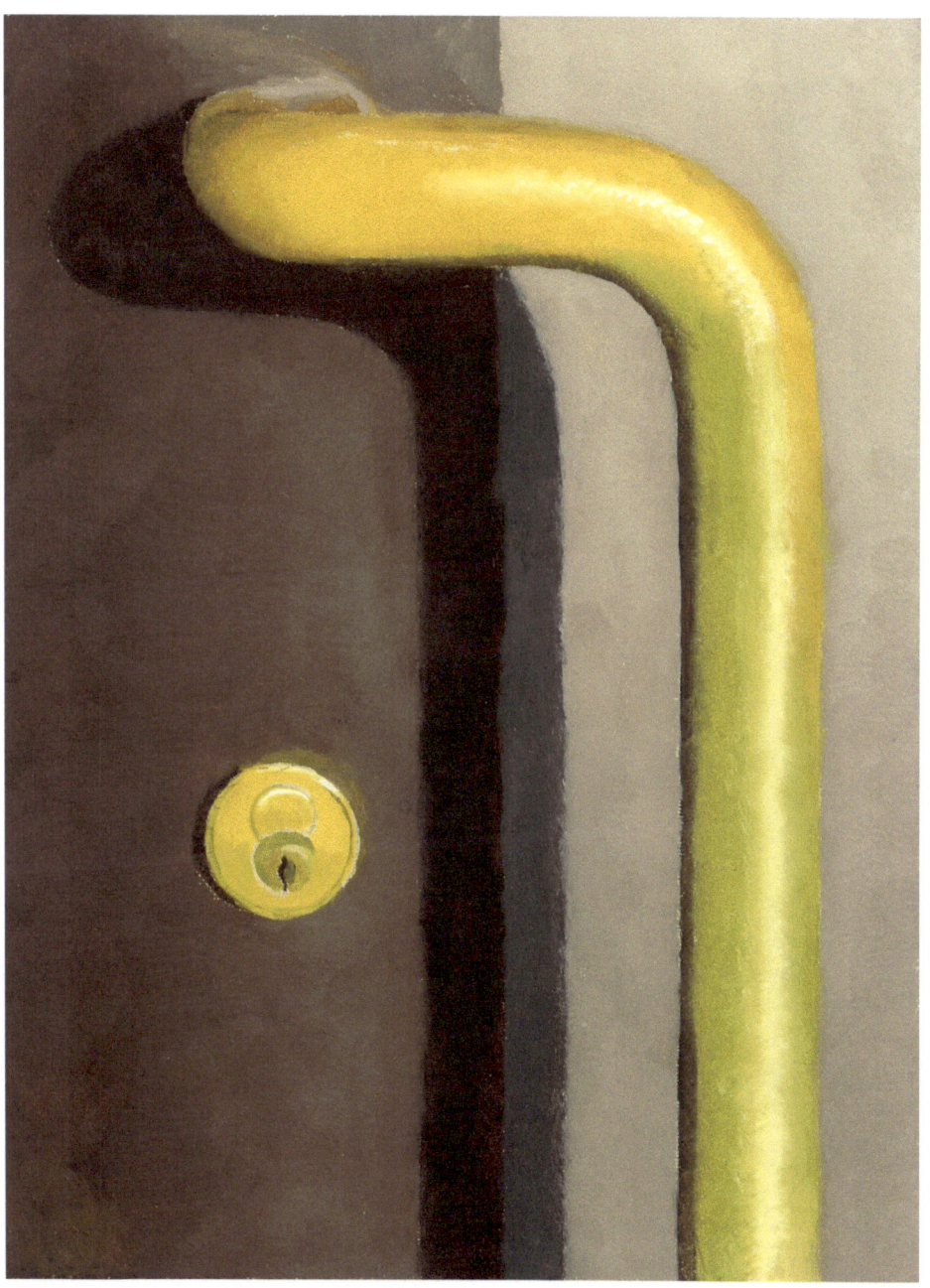

Too often, the opportunity knocks, but by the time you push back the chain,
push back the bolt, unhook the two locks and shut off the burglar alarm, it's too late.
Rita Coolidge

# GIRL CROSSING

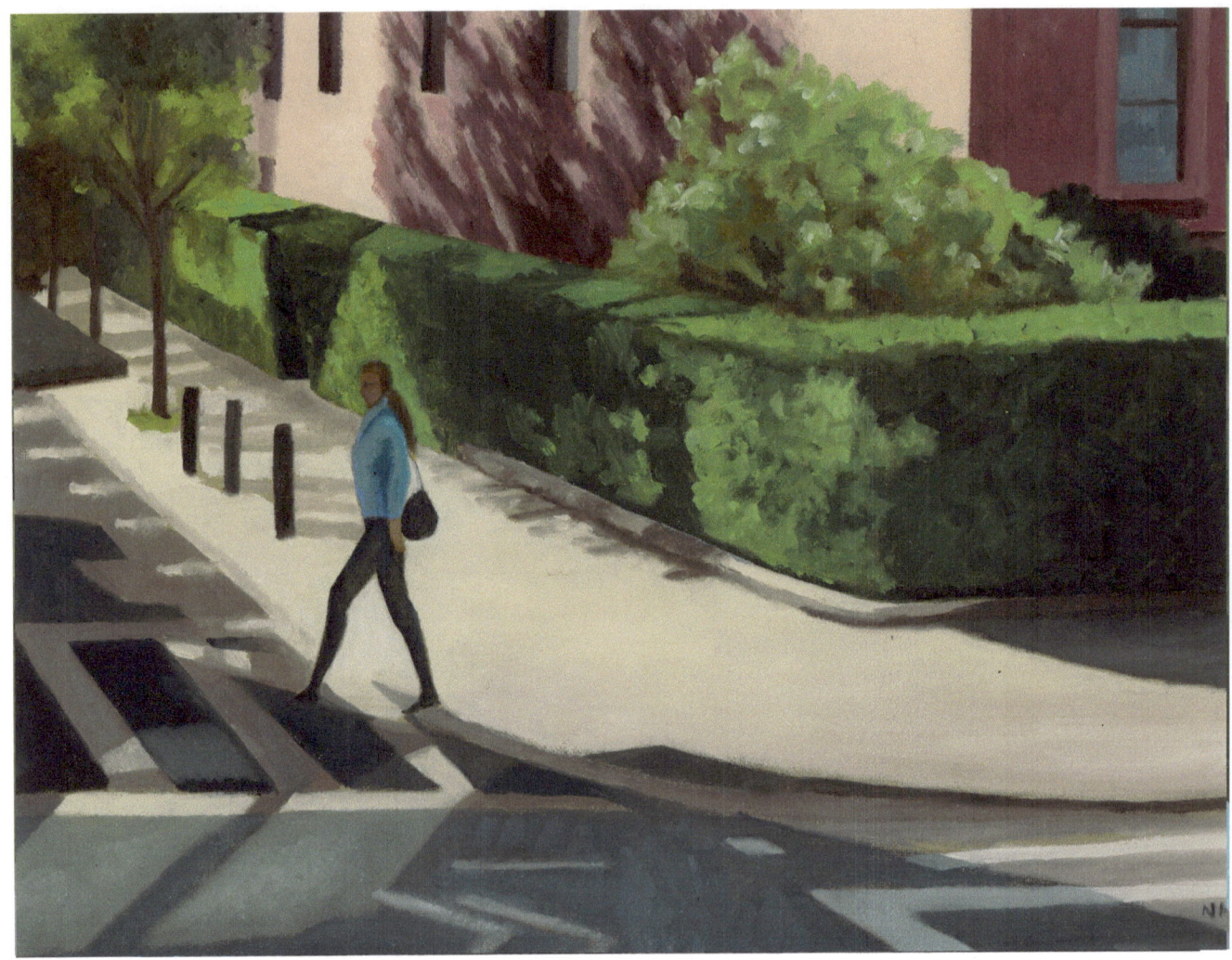

Brooklyn is full of people going places in a hurry.

# WOMAN AND DOG ON THE CORNER

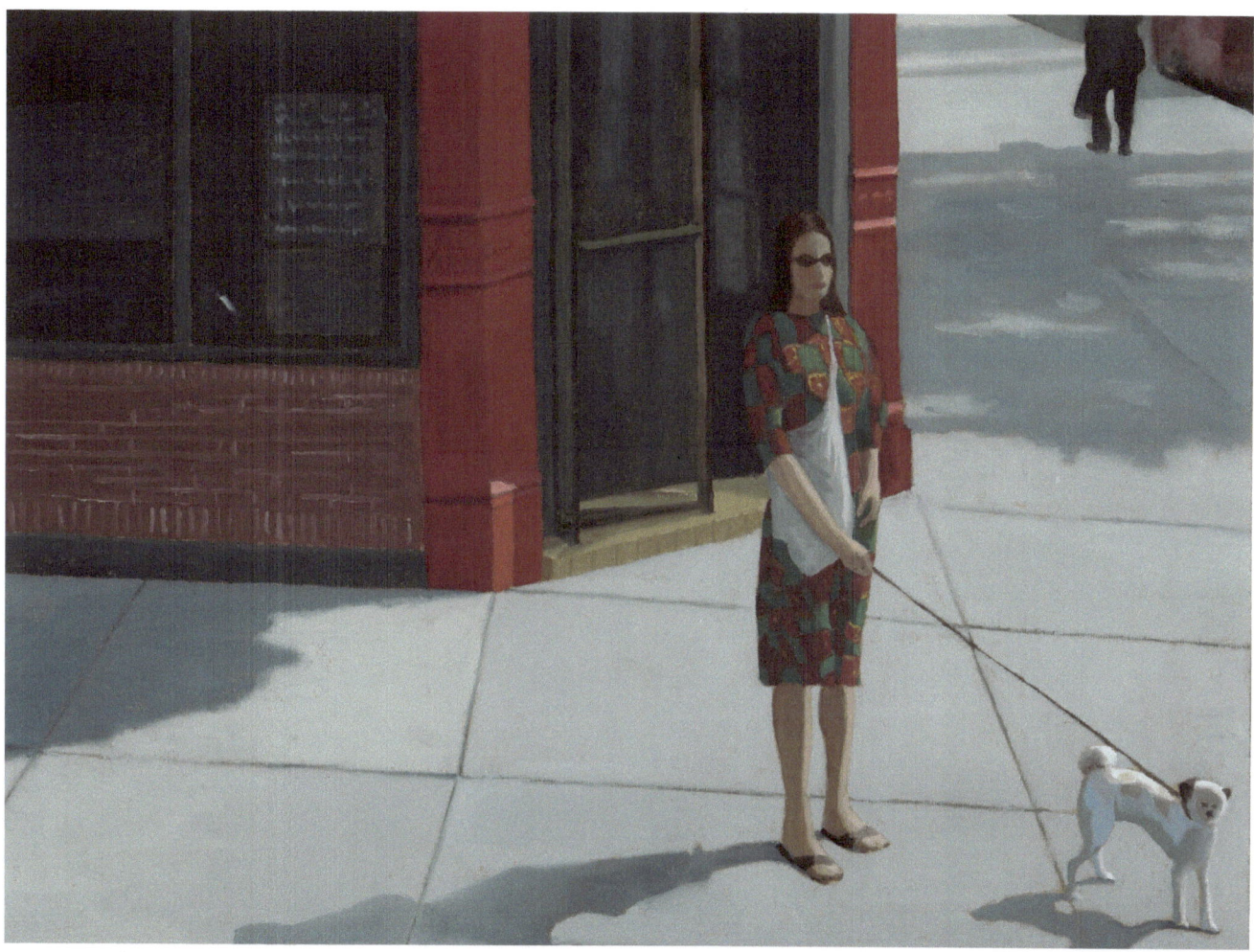

This woman will be standing on this corner in Parkslope in her flowered dress
 with her little dog forever, and the man in black will never get where he is
going.  Such is the power of a painting or snapshot.  We look back at
pictures we have saved and they become our memories in ways so subtle
we don't even notice.

# THE YELLOW DOOR

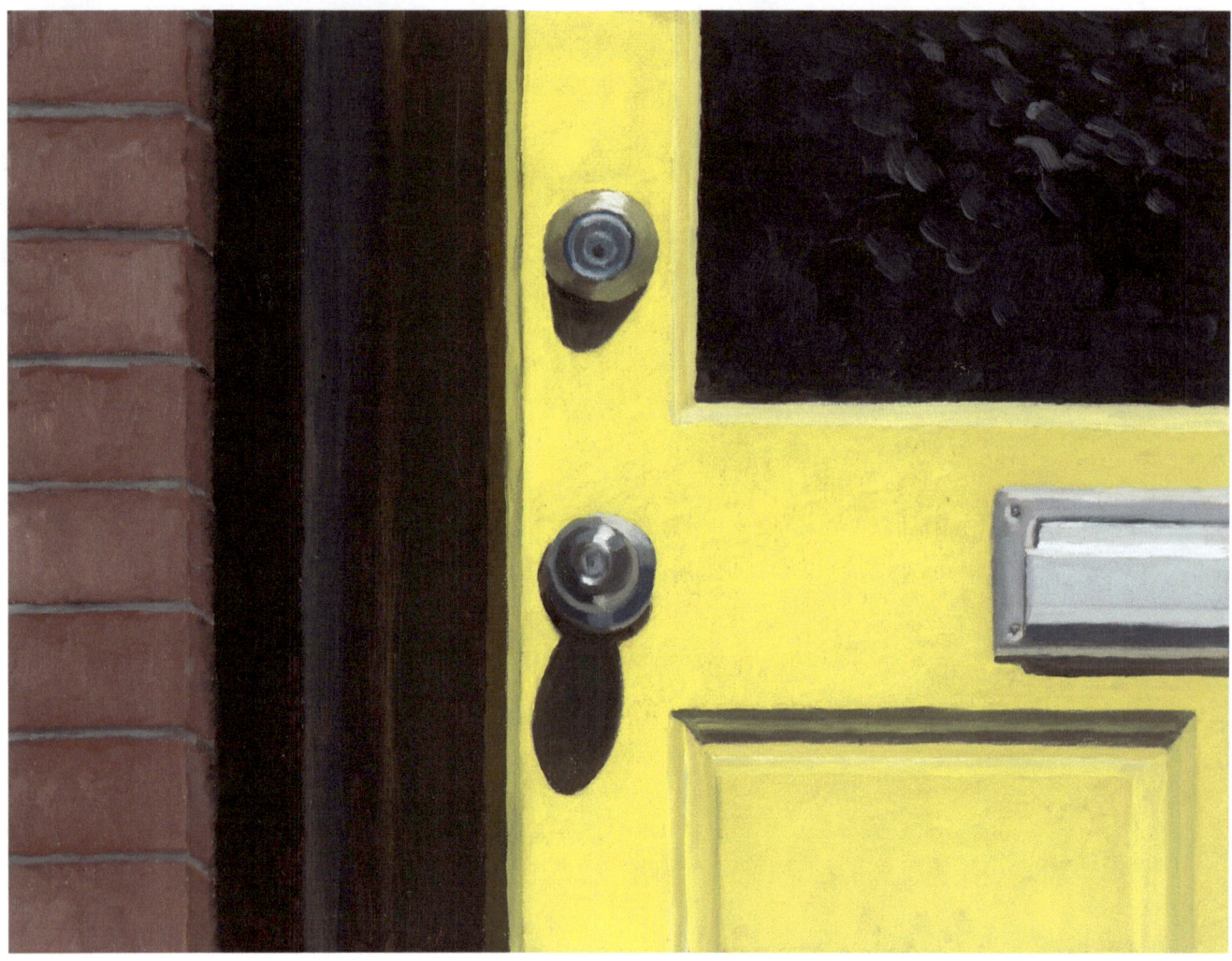

"Not knowing when the dawn will come, I open every door"
Emily Dickenson

# THE RED DOOR

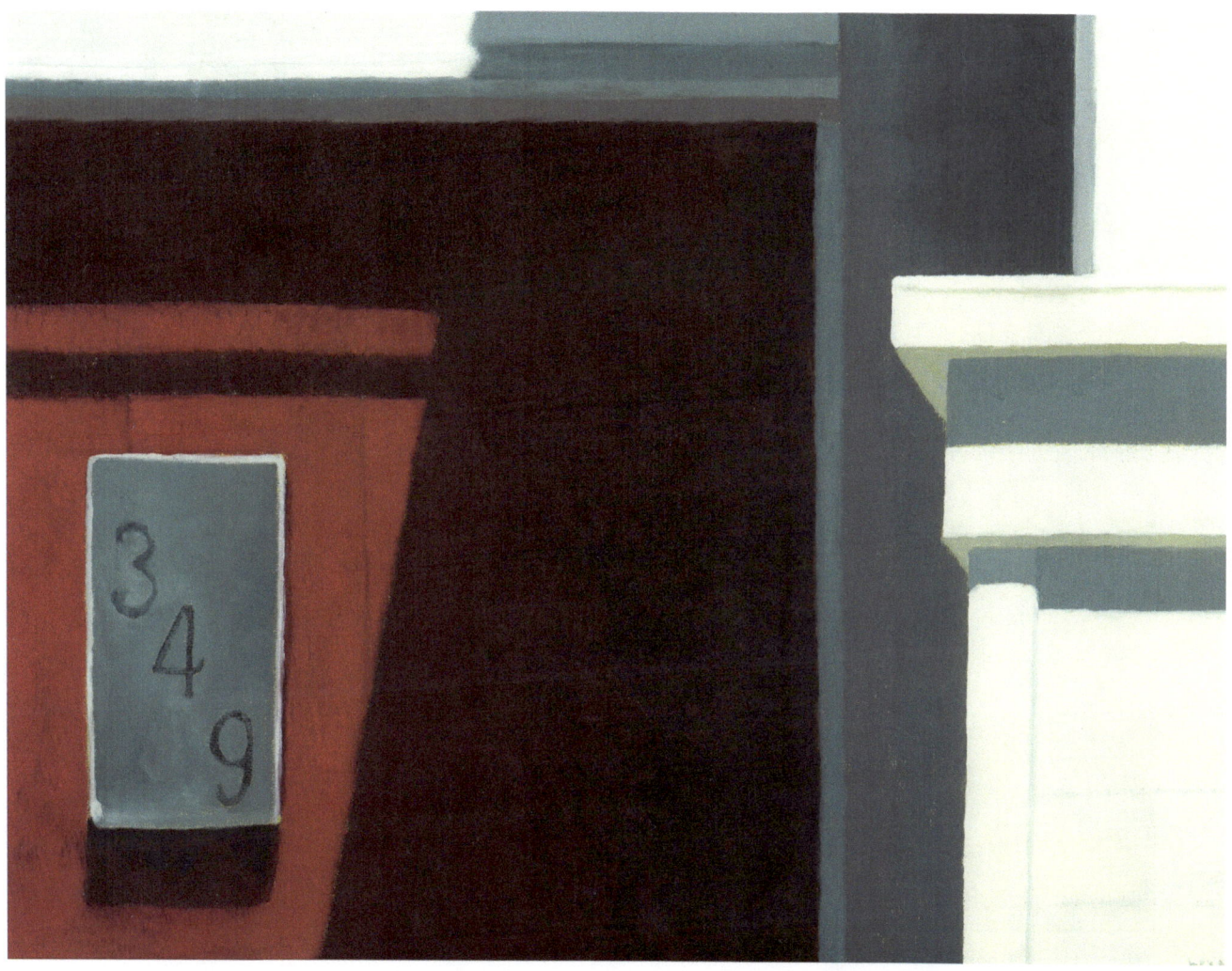

Who lives at 349 and why did they paint their door red?

# DOOR KNOCKER ON 6TH AVENUE

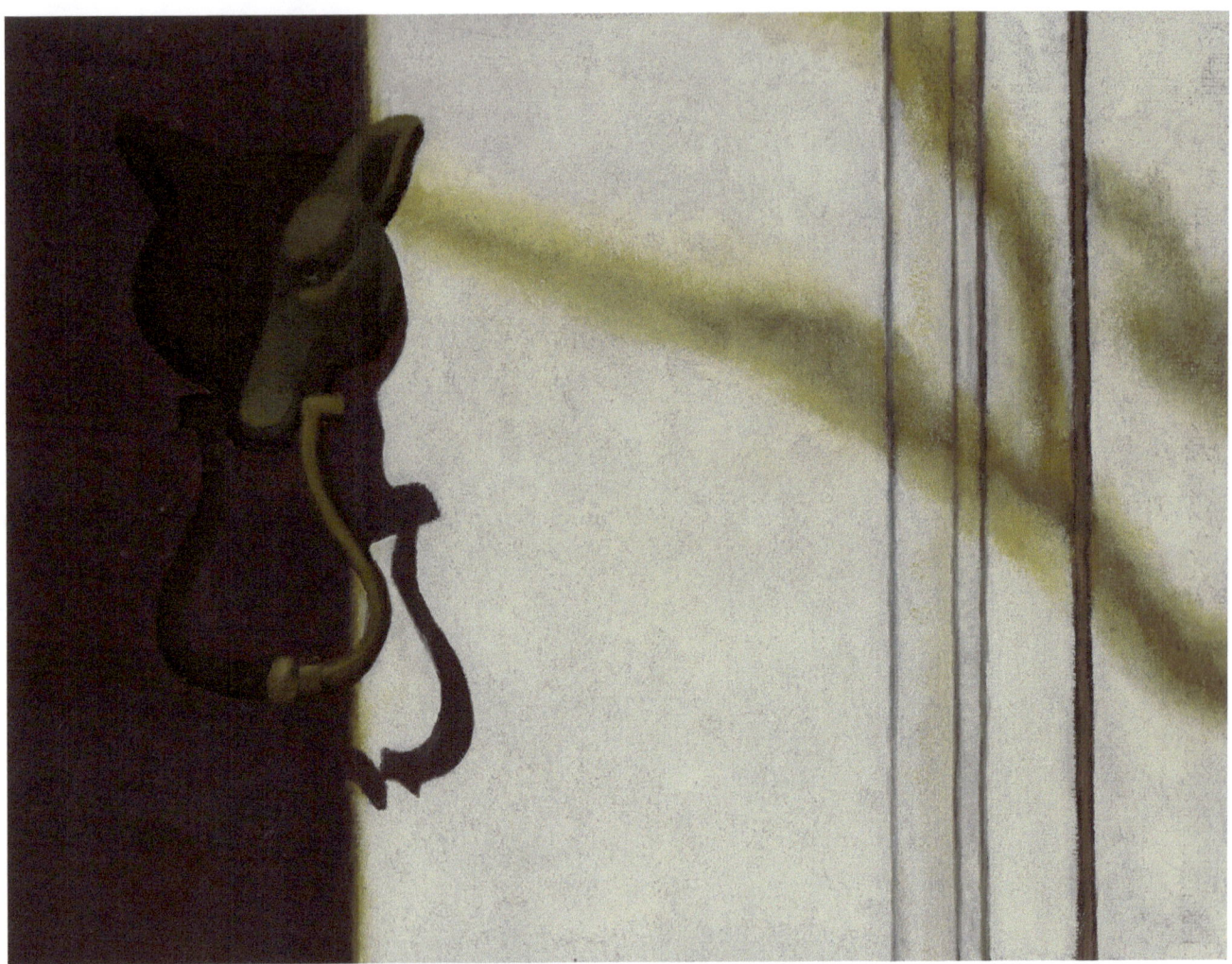

This door knocker seems to be saying, "I dare you to use me".  A wonderful mixed message found on 6th Avenue.  Who lives there, I wonder, a fortune teller, sorceress, or little old lady with a good sense of humor?

# BROOKLYN BRIDGE

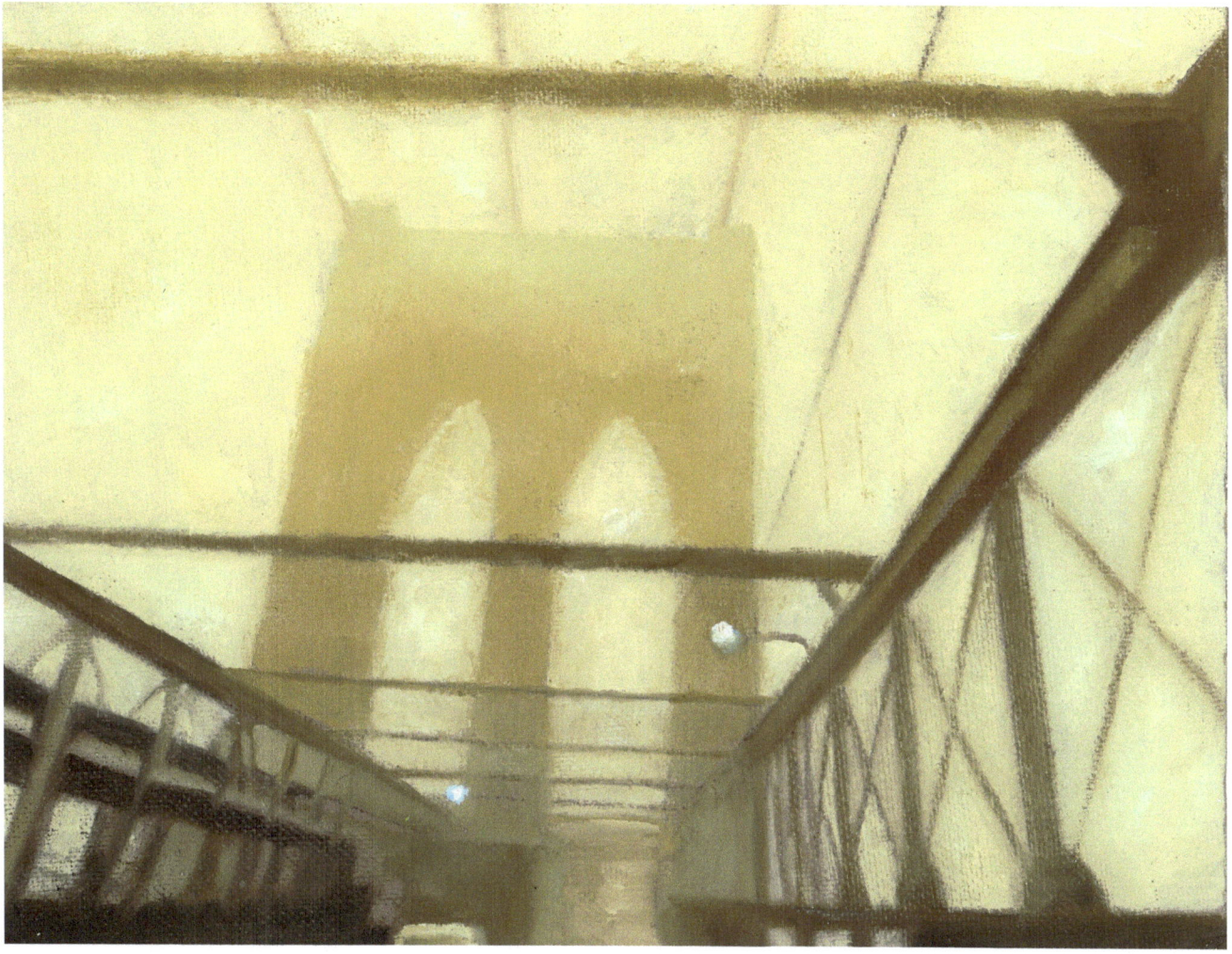

This painting was created to be a part of my video THE DREAM,
The DREAM can be found on my youtube channel here.
https://youtu.be/_51WW5ehlKI

# BACK YARD FENCE

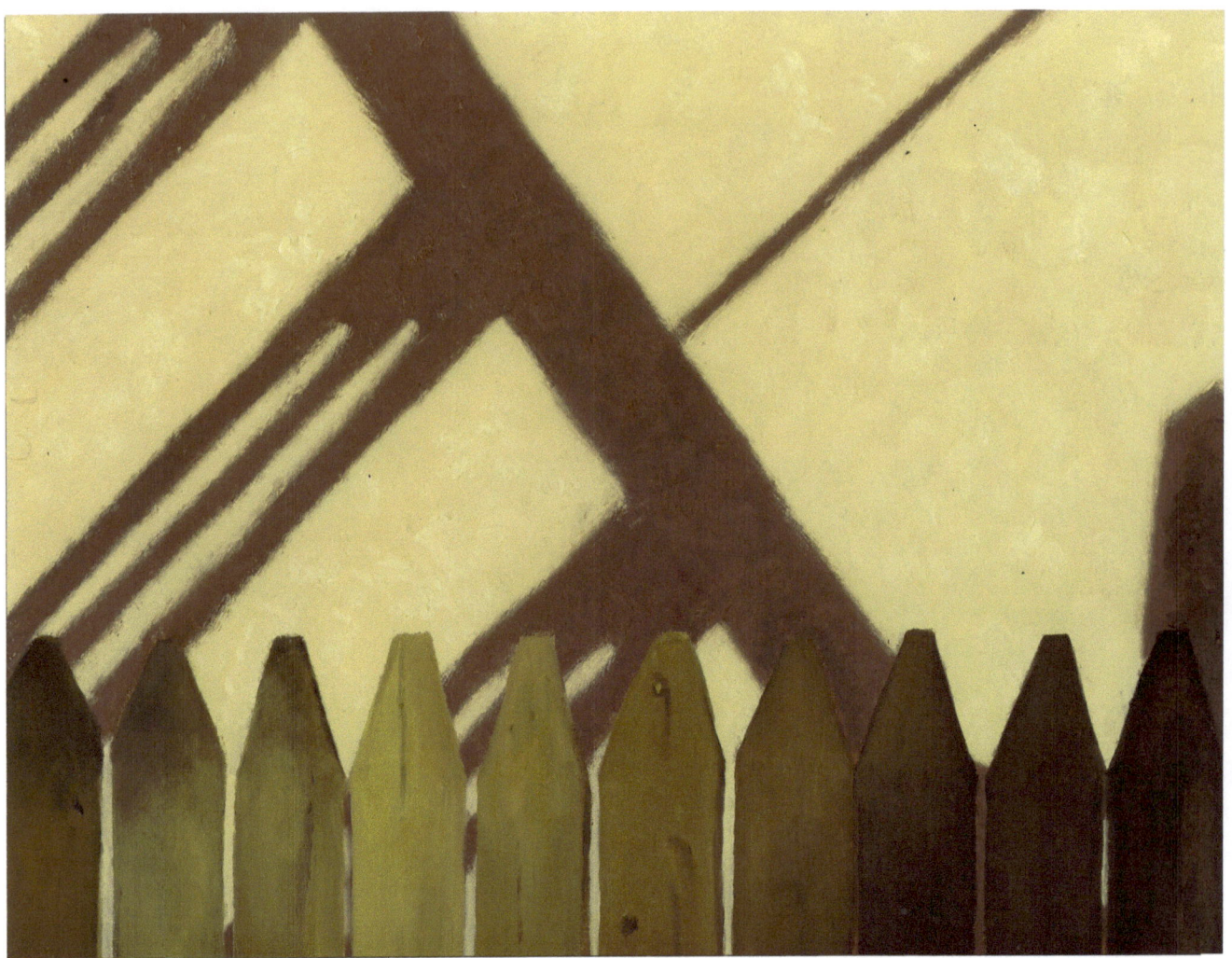

This fence, dancing in and out of the light, catches my eye as I sit in my daughter's Parkslope backyard. Architectural shadows pierce the picture plane in striking ways, darting here and there uniting shapes in ever changing patterns.

# UPSTAIRS

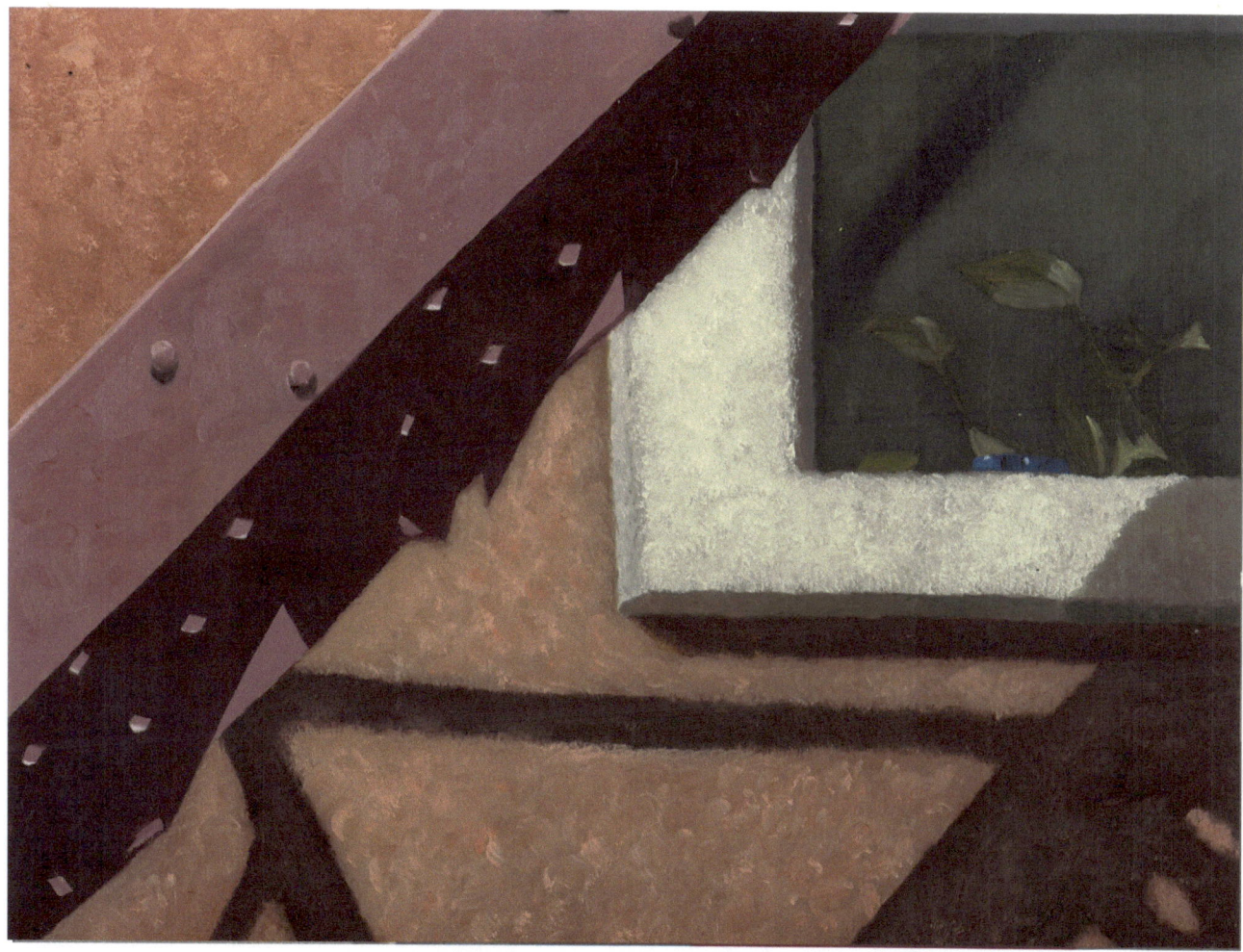

While sitting on the back porch I look up into the window of my oldest grandson and his wife's apartment. I am so glad the family lives near each other. It is such a gift.

# GHOST IN PROSPECT PARK

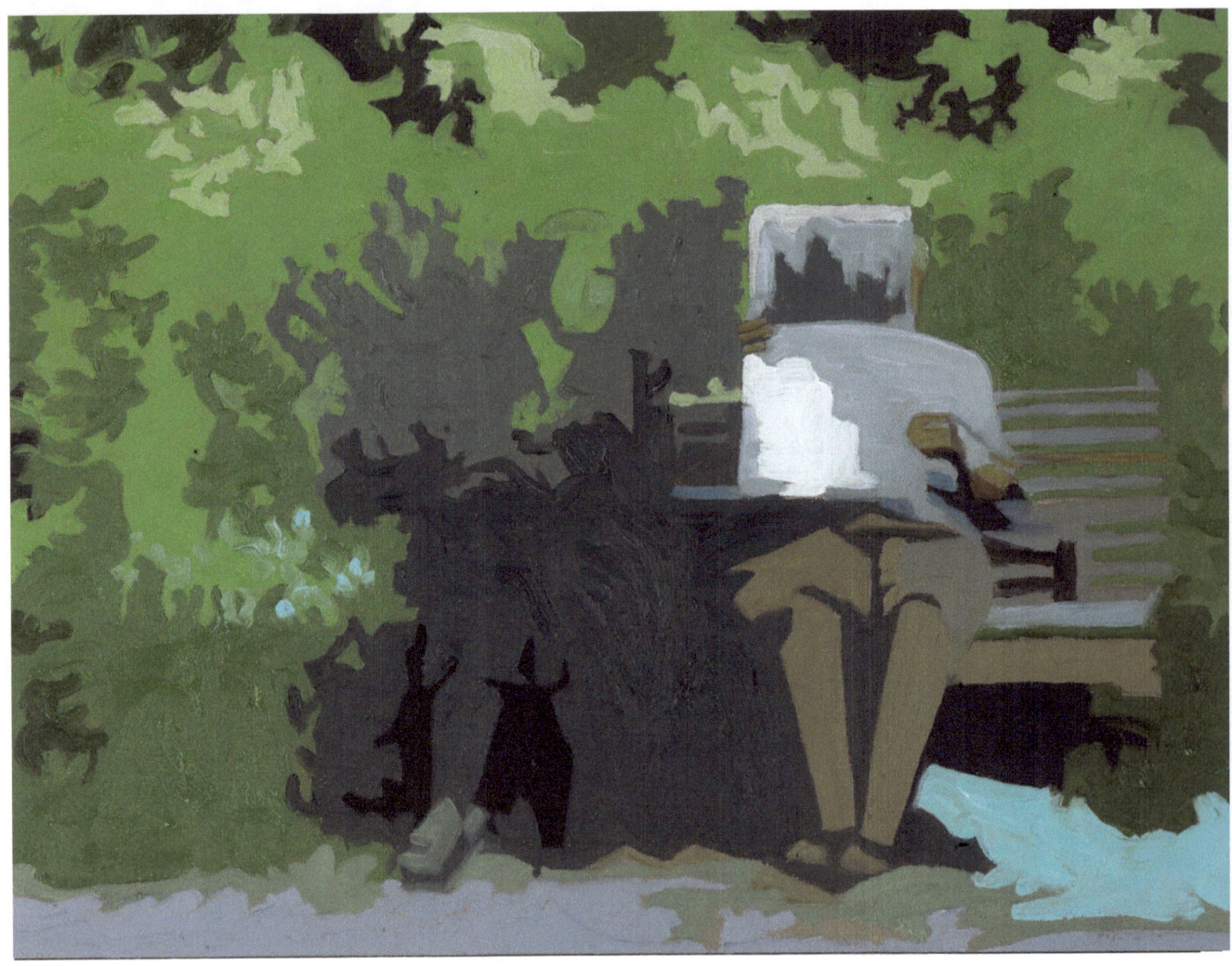

Sometimes one senses the presense of someone when noone is there.
This happens to me sometimes.  Not sure what to make of it.

# STROLL BY PROSPECT PARK

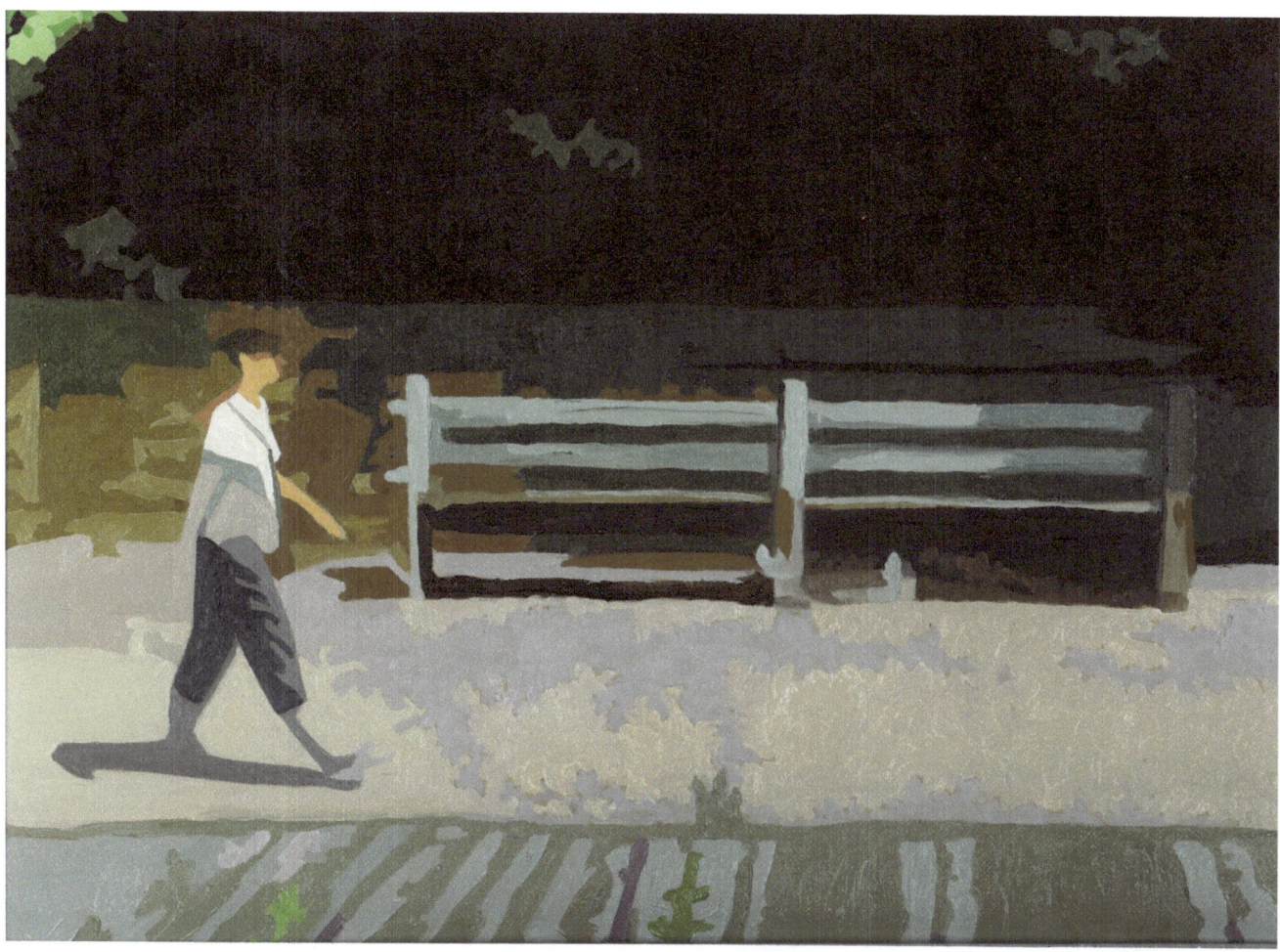

585 acres of beautiful park land is certainly one of the best reasons to live in Brooklyn.

# THE BLUES ABOUT THE NEWS

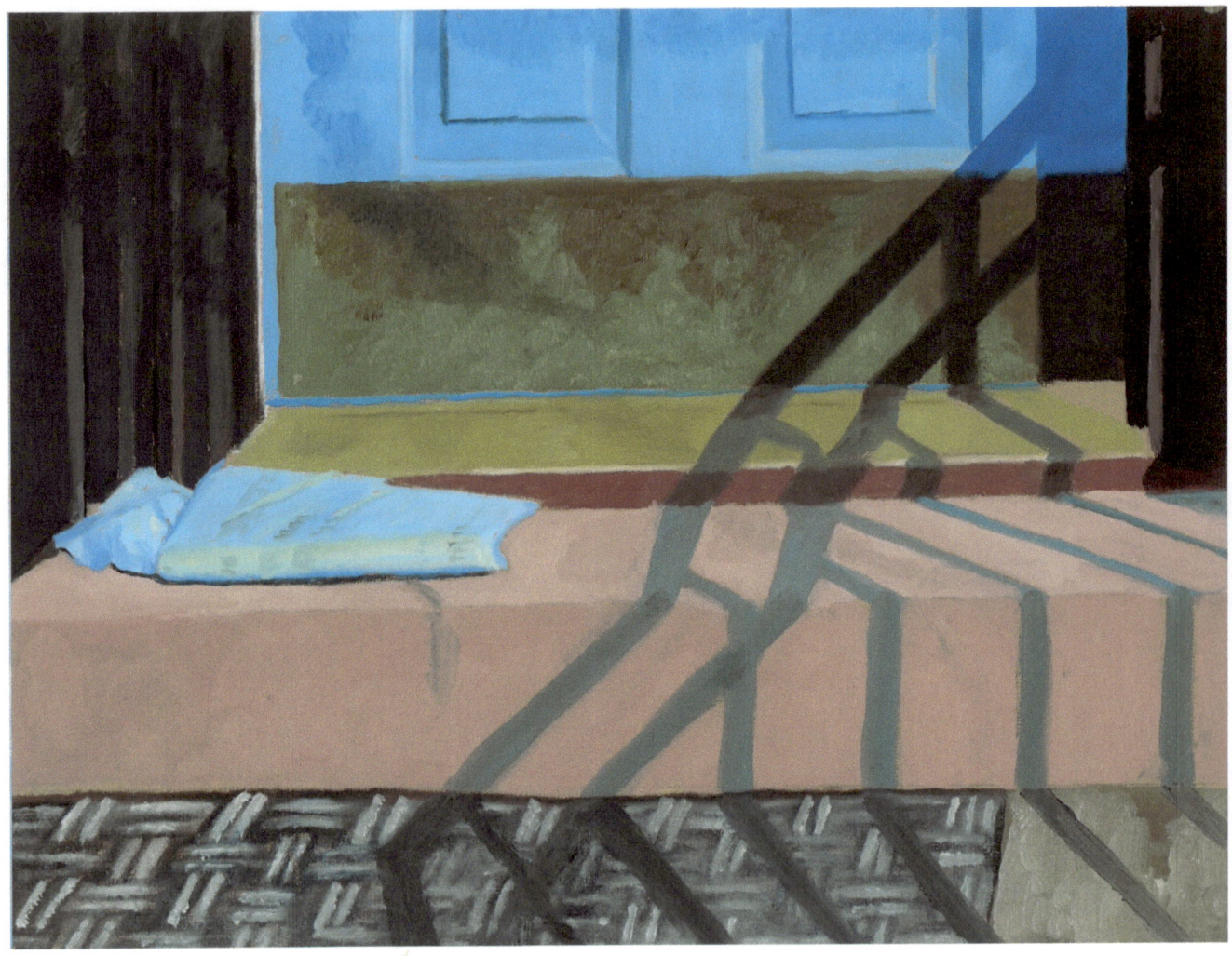

Will the morning newspaper go the way of 78 records, glass milk jars, Hoola Hoops, the Twist, the old Penn Station and Lil Abner?

# MORNING AFTER SNOW

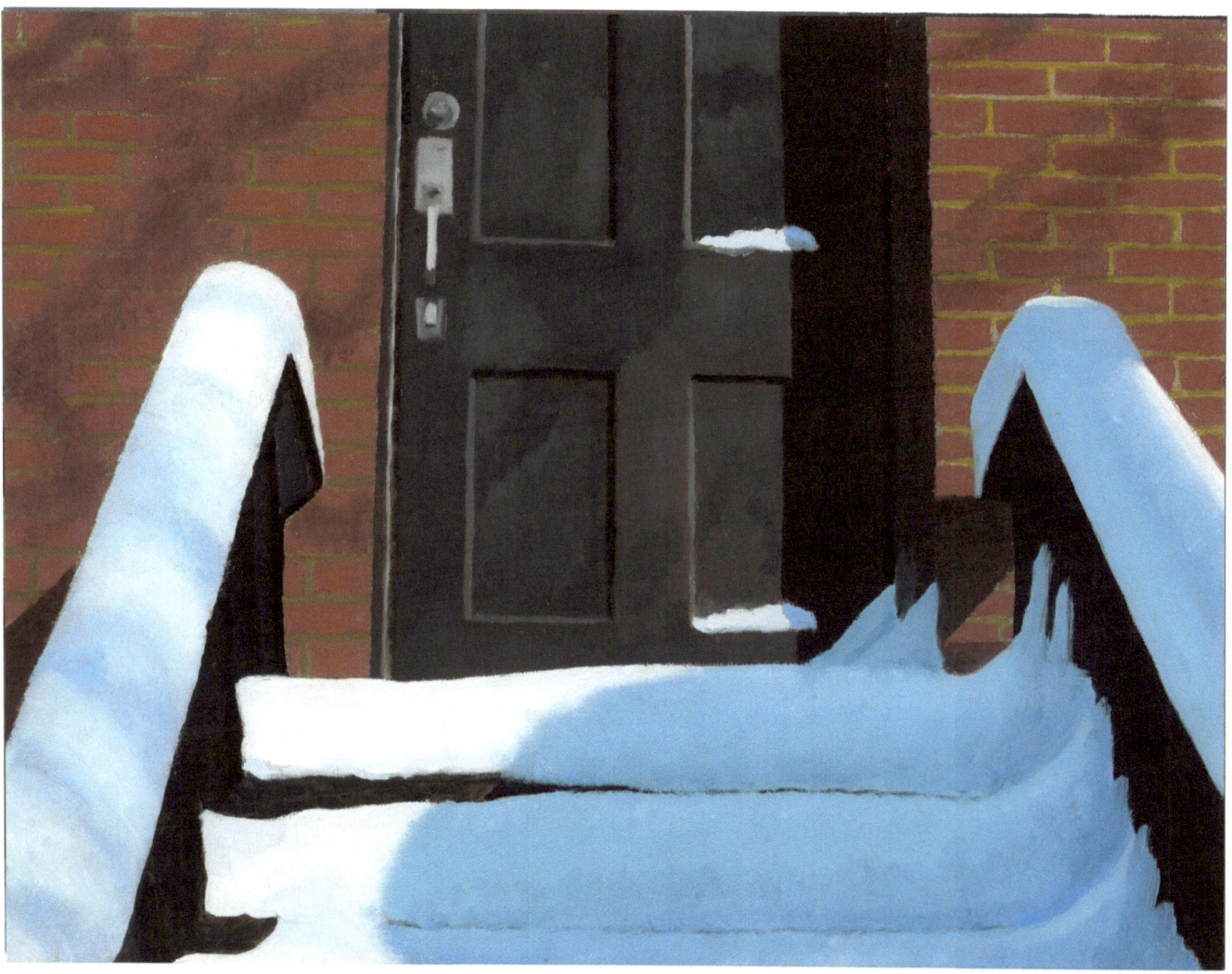

I love the morning after a snow storm when no footprints, except the bird's and the squirrel's, mar the pure rounded sculpture the snow creates.
This Sunday morning in Brooklyn no one has even opened the door to see what's out there.

# MONDAY MORNING 8:30

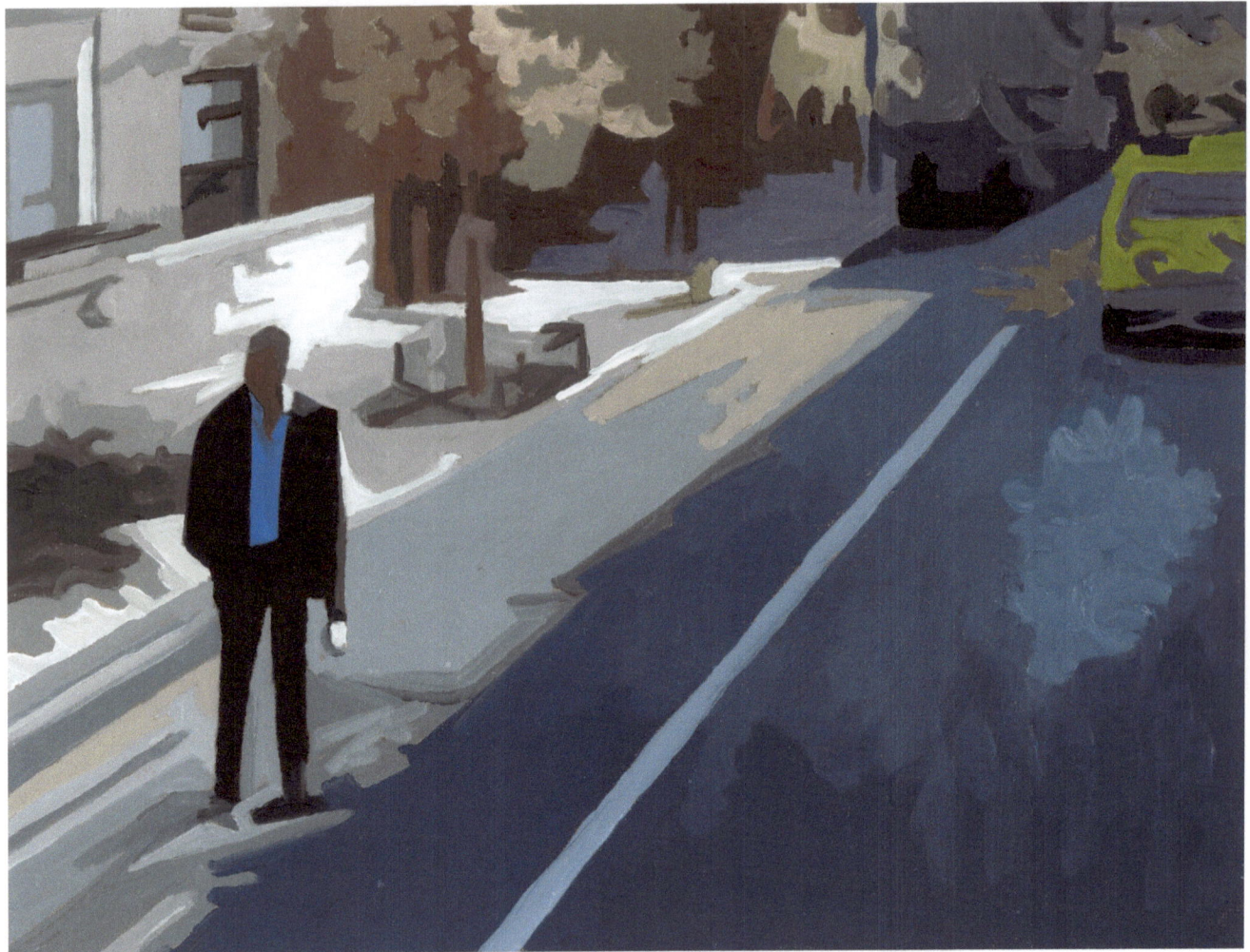

This guy, waiting for a ride with his lunch in his hand looks ready for the week ahead.

# FRIDAY AFTERNOON 5:00

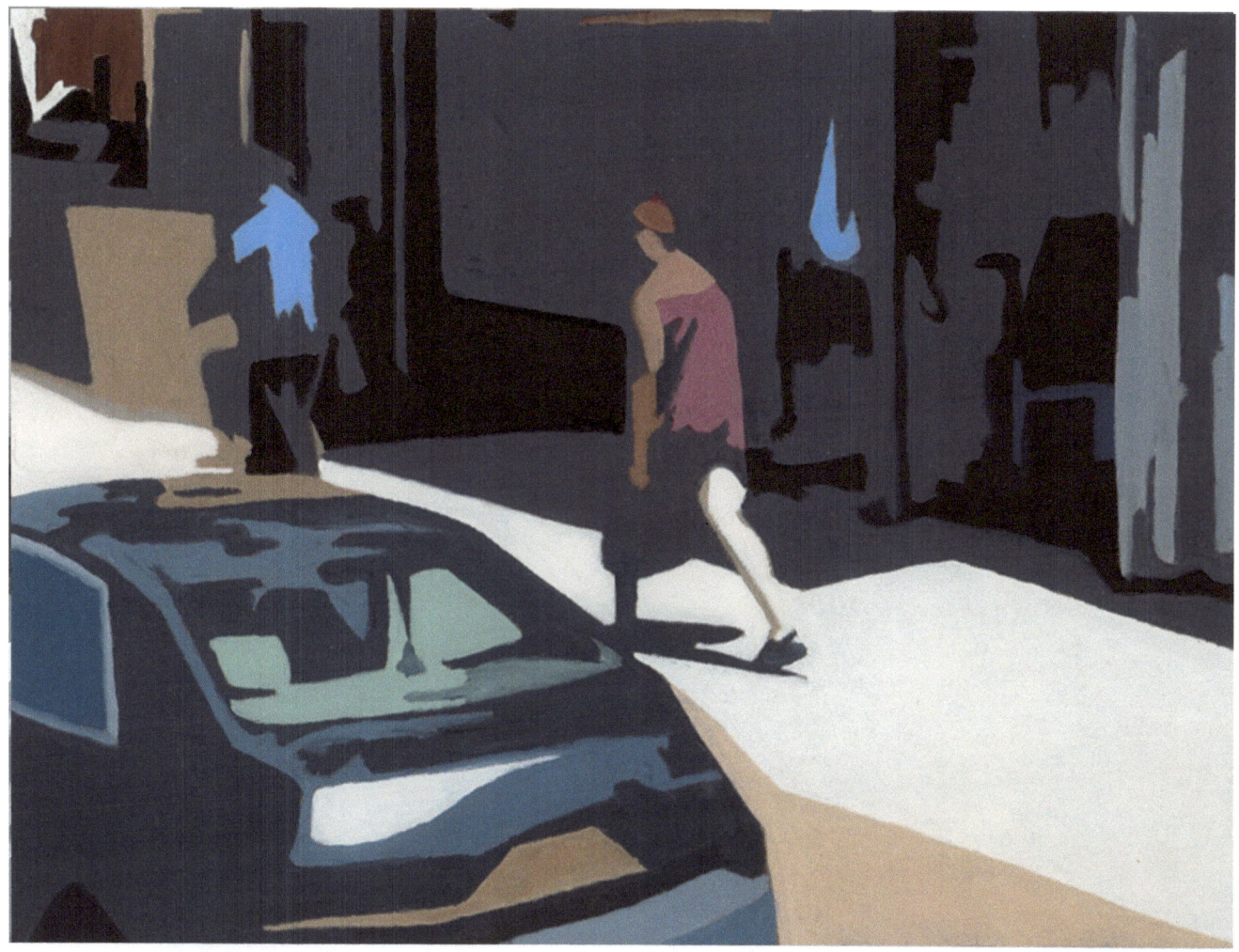

Caught in the angles of the here and now, the great rush at five to escape work and get home.

# PIZZA MAN

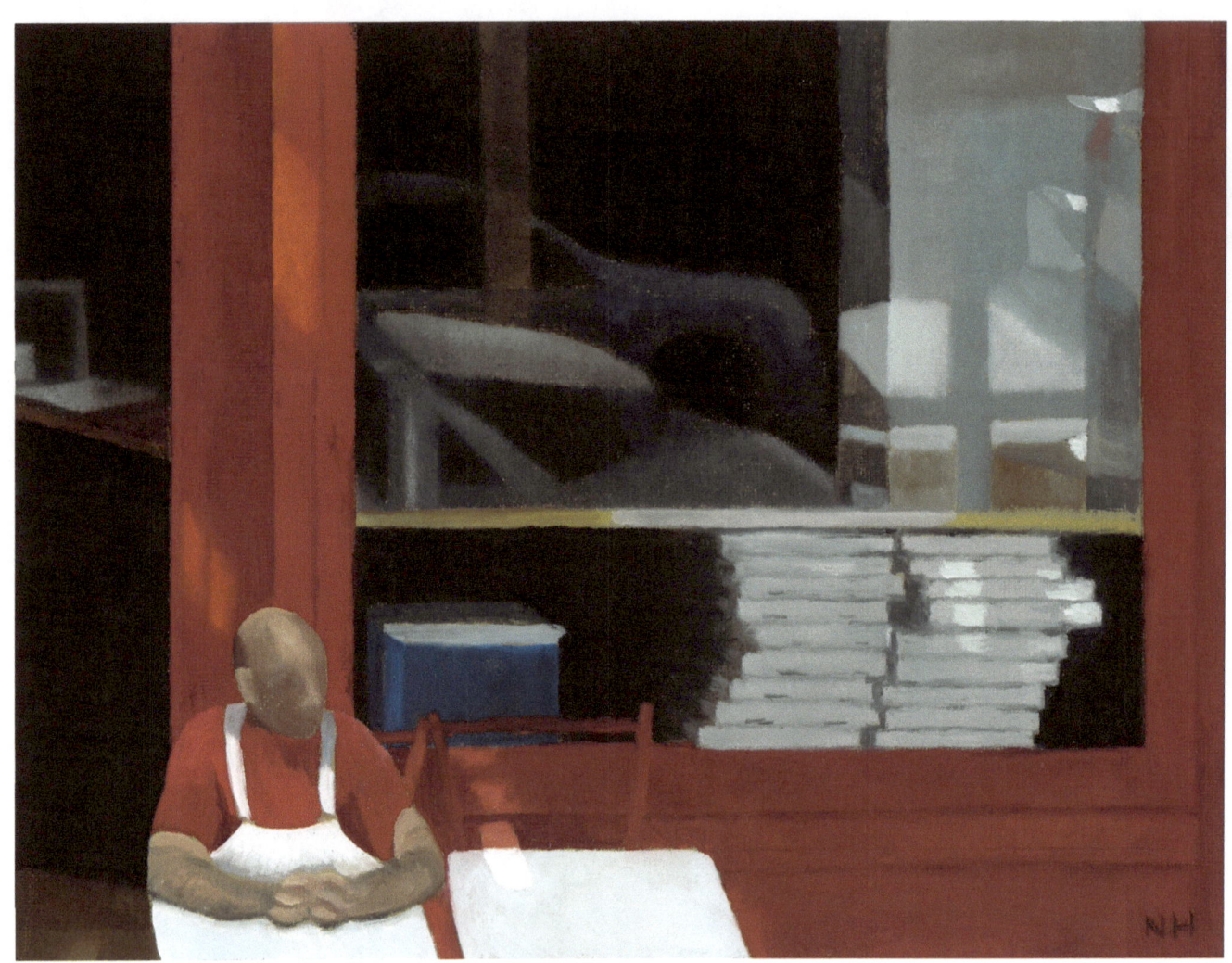

# RED TRUCK ON SEVENTH AVENUE

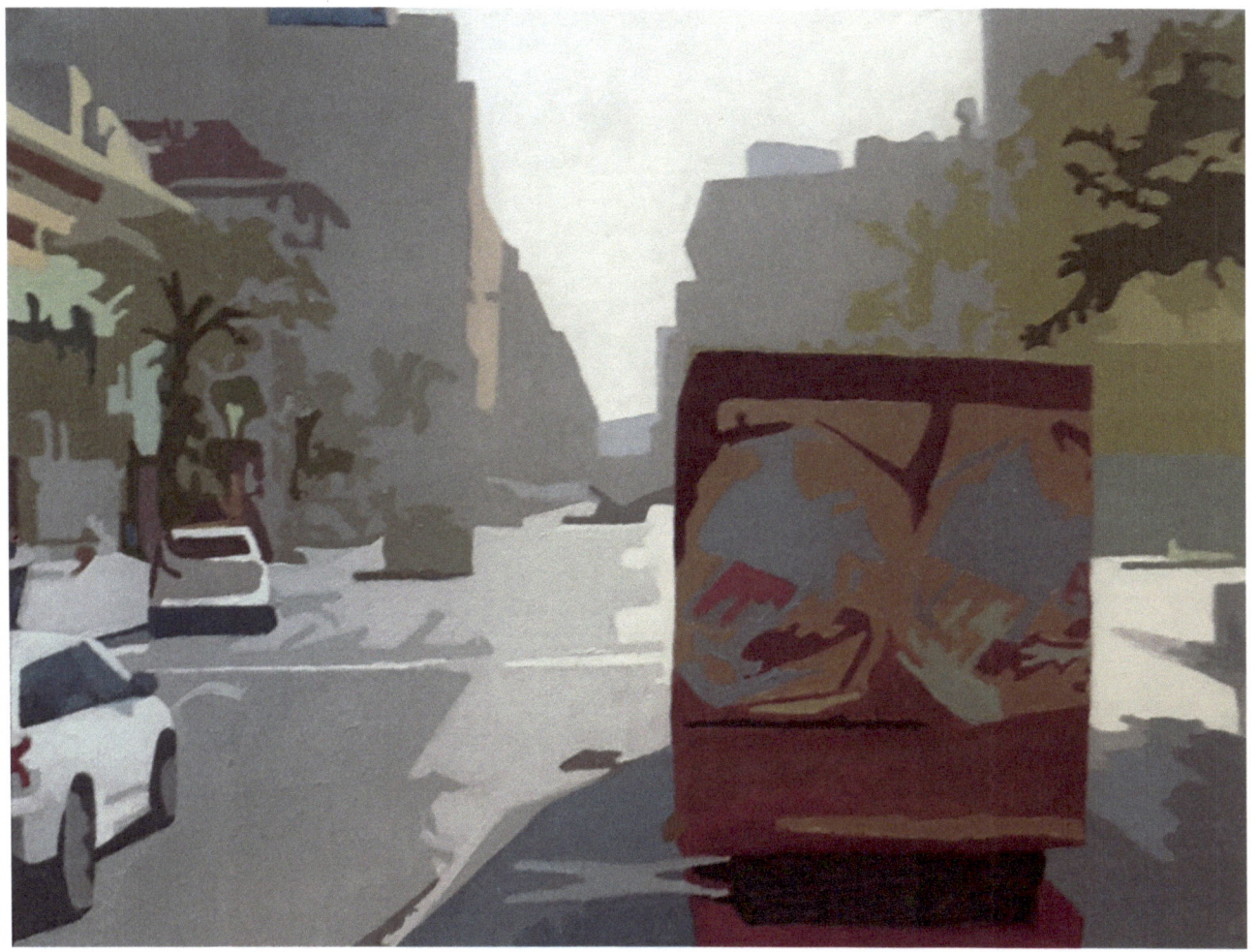

# CROSSING

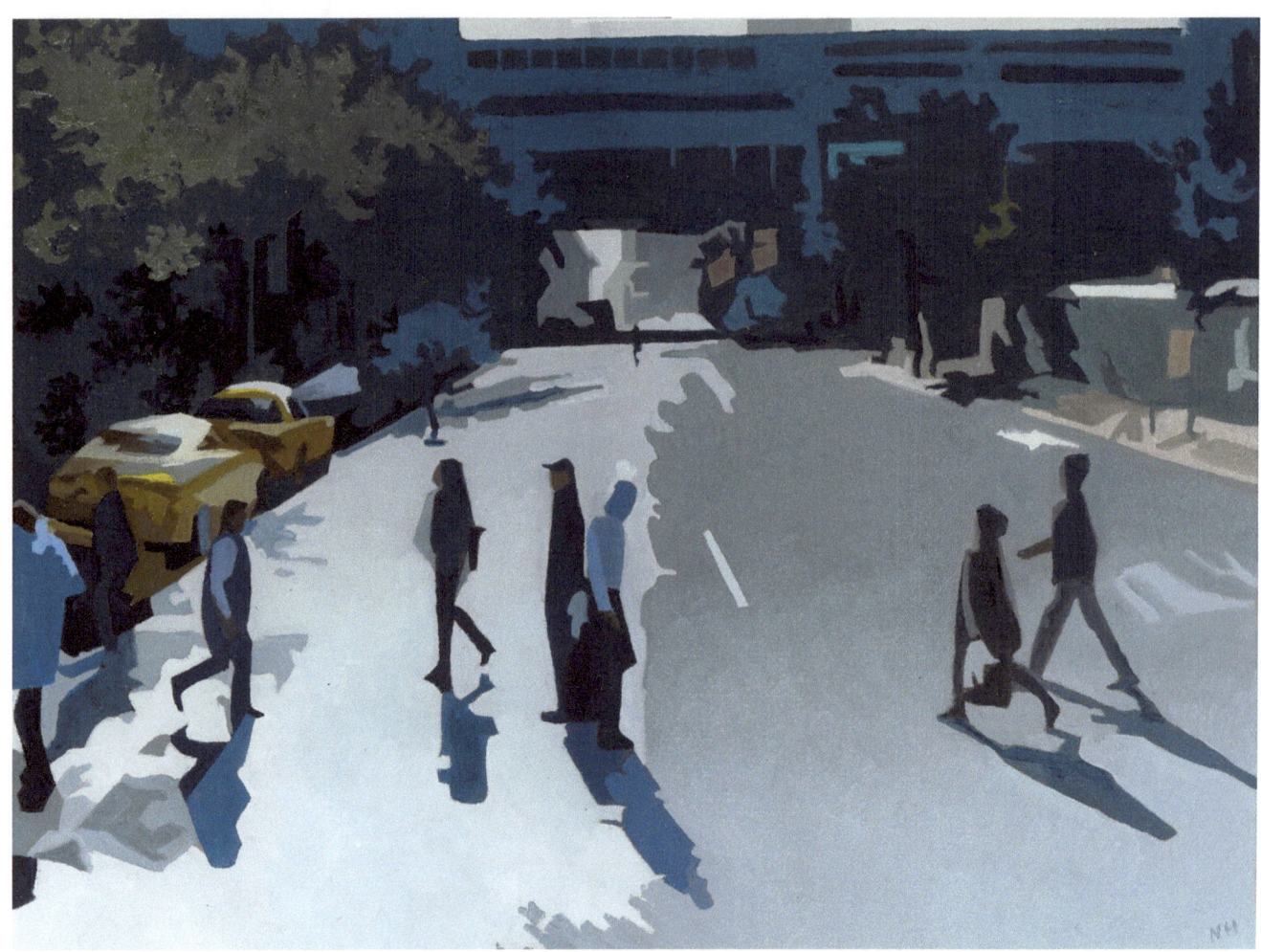

I have often wondered how living in the hard edges of the city affects people.

# CAUGHT ON THE CORNER

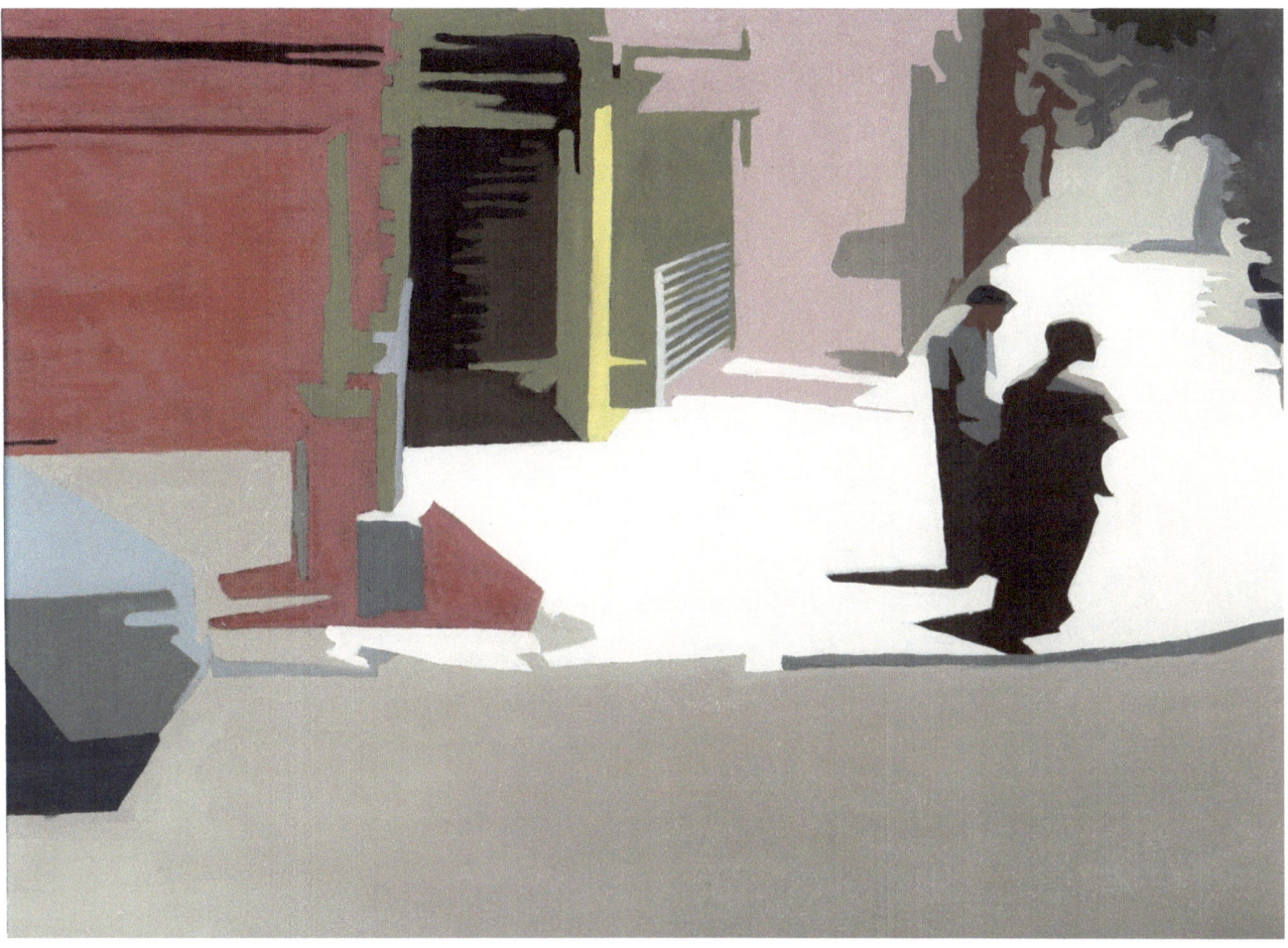

Here the city has carved out pieces of the men who are caught forever waiting on the corner for an oportunity to escape.

OUT OF THE SUBWAY INTO THE SUN

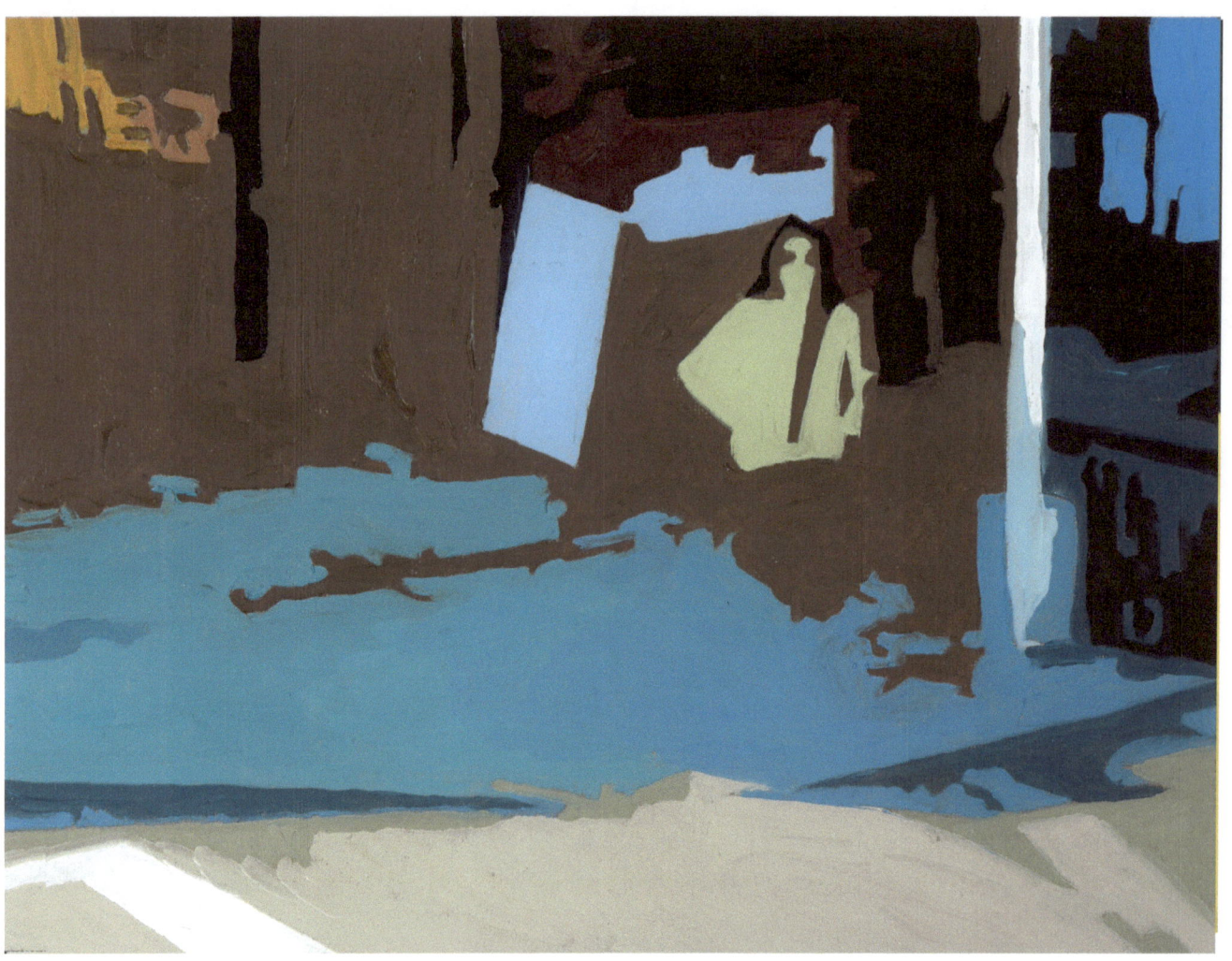

These paintings were completed over a period of a few years.

As you may have noticed the style of painting changes from

being a nostalgic  sort of realism to a hard edged take on city life.

I have arranged them that way but they were not necessarily

painted in that order.  I try to paint the way I feel about the subject.

I am, like the woman in the painting SUNGLASSES IN THE CITY,

who is emerging from the subway into the glare and confusion of

the city, tyring to make visual and emotional sense of my quick

impressions of Brooklyn.

If you would like to subscribe to my blog and get a painting

as they are created  you can find it here:

http://postcardsfromthemainline.blogspot.com

A large selection of my work can be found here:

www.nancyherman.com